..AT PRAY

SOMEONE WHO READ THIS BOOK SAID, "OF ALL THE *Prayer Warrior* series, this is the book the devil hates the most!"

I believe it. This book will undoubtedly help more people become personally involved in the great worldwide prayer movement than the other three combined. And the devil has good reason to hate it, because he knows what damage a highly motivated and well-organized prayer army can do and will do to his domain of evil!

C. Peter Wagner

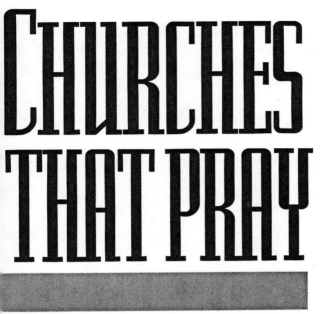

CHURCHES THAT PRAY

C. PETER WAGNER

CHURCHES THAT PRAY

HOW PRAYER CAN HELP REVITALIZE YOUR CONGREGATION AND BREAK DOWN THE WALLS BETWEEN YOUR CHURCH AND YOUR COMMUNITY

Regal Books
A Division of Gospel Light
Ventura, California, U.S.A.

Published by Regal Books
A Division of Gospel Light
Ventura, California, U.S.A.
Printed in U.S.A.

Regal Books is a ministry of Gospel Light, an evangelical Christian publisher dedicated to serving the local church. We believe God's vision for Gospel Light is to provide church leaders with biblical, user-friendly materials that will help them evangelize, disciple and minister to children, youth and families.

It is our prayer that this Regal Book will help you discover biblical truth for your own life and help you meet the needs of others. May God richly bless you.

For a free catalog of resources from Regal Books/Gospel Light please contact your Christian supplier or call 1-800-4-GOSPEL.

Library of Congress Cataloging-in-Publication Data

Wagner, C. Peter.
    Churches that pray : how prayer can help revitalize your congregation and break down the walls between your church and your community / C. Peter Wagner.
    p.   cm.
    ISBN 0-8307-1658-0 (trade)
    1. Prayer groups. 2. Church renewal. 3. Mission of the church.
I. Title.
BV287.W34   1993   93-5420
248.3'2—dc20   CIP

3 4 5 6 7 8 9 10 11 12 13 14 15 16 17 18 19 20 / 00 99 98 97 96 95

Rights for publishing this book in other languages are contracted by Gospel Literature International (GLINT). GLINT also provides technical help for the adaptation, translation, and publishing of Bible study resources and books in scores of languages worldwide. For further information, contact GLINT, Post Office Box 4060, Ontario, California, 91761-1003, U.S.A., or the publisher.

LOVINGLY DEDICATED
TO MY MOTHER AND FATHER
C. GRAHAM WAGNER
PHYLLIS H. WAGNER

Contents

Introduction

T HIS FOURTH BOOK IN THE *PRAYER WARRIOR* SERIES WAS originally meant to be the first. When I began researching the prayer movement in 1987, I found three key areas that had not been addressed to any significant extent in the vast literature on prayer: (1) prayer and the local church; (2) intercession for Christian leaders; and (3) strategic-level intercession. As a longtime professor of church growth, I planned to begin with the first area.

But I soon became aware that I was not able to get a start on exploring the prayer ministry of local churches or the relationship of prayer to church growth. I did not know exactly why. So I wrote *Warfare Prayer* first, then *Prayer Shield*. Before I could start this book, I became so impressed by the urgent need for a book on spiritual mapping that I turned the series of three into four and edited *Breaking Strongholds in Your City.*

By then, I was prepared for God to show me clearly why He had not allowed me to write *Churches That Pray* sooner. It was because I was working on only half of the correct premise. I was about to write an entire book on prayer within the local church. Although this was good and greatly needed in a book such as this, it was much more recently that I realized what I should deal with in the other half of this book.

As much as anything else, the words I heard from Pastor Jack Graham of Prestonwood Baptist Church in Dallas, Texas, completed my partial thinking. Jack said, quite prophetically I believe, "Revival will come when we get the walls down between the church and the community."

This was it!

Yes, churches must pray longer, harder and more effectively within their own walls. But they also should be praying in the community outside the church. My research on the prayer movement had surfaced methods of praying in the community and I immediately saw how the two would fit together.

The first five chapters focus on the prayer movement, the nature of prayer and prayer in the church. The last five chapters highlight the need to pray in the community through praise marches, prayerwalks, prayer expeditions and prayer journeys. Together, they have the potential to make prayer one of the most stimulating and productive ministries of your church.

The Great Prayer Movement

E

I WAS ATTENDING THE MASSIVE LAUSANNE II CONGRESS ON World Evangelization in Manila in 1989. My decades of experience in such meetings led me to the conclusion that frequently the most important things happen in corridors and over coffee breaks rather than in plenary sessions. So that day I was being rather naughty by skipping the plenary session.

I worked for a couple of hours in my hotel room, then went over to the display section of the convention center. I bought a Coke and prayed in an audible whisper, "Lord, please let me talk to the person you select." Then I wandered into the bookstore.

My friend Jim Montgomery was there, and I wondered, *Lord, why Jim?* He is my neighbor and we see each other almost every week in our Sunday School class in Pasadena, California. I do not have to travel halfway around the world to see Jim.

"YOU'RE THE SPEAKER!"

Jim opened the conversation by saying, "We have an excellent registration for the luncheon." I did not know what luncheon he might be talking about until he told me that it was a major event scheduled to inform and motivate leaders from many nations of the world about the Discipling a Whole Nation (DAWN) movement, which he heads. Not only that, but I was to be the major speaker! Furthermore, it was to begin in less than two hours! Somehow, that assignment, which I had agreed to months previously, had not found its way onto my schedule.

First I said, "I'll be there."

Then I said, "Thank you, Lord."

That incident itself would have satisfied me for a morning of answered prayer, but it was not over. Before I left, I began chatting with Rey Halili, a Filipino bookstore manager. He shared that in the Philippines my books were too expensive because Regal Books was not in a position to grant English rights to Philippine publishers to publish them locally instead of importing them. I told him I would look into it.

WHERE IS GEORGALYN?

When I left the bookstore, I headed up the stairs to a huge public lounge where coffee breaks were held. I realized that the one person I needed to see about the Philippine books was Georgalyn Wilkinson who heads Gospel Literature International (GLINT). I knew she was attending the congress, but I had not spoken to her and had no idea where she was staying or what her activities might be. To hope to run into her among those 4,500 delegates was far from a reasonable expectation. So again I prayed audibly, "Lord, please let me see Georgalyn."

I was heading for the lounge to be by myself so I could prepare for my luncheon address at the DAWN meeting. I was relieved when I saw not a soul in the lounge, except for two people obviously in a business-type meeting halfway across the room. Then, when I looked more closely, I could hardly believe what I saw—one of them was Georgalyn Wilkinson!

"Thank you, Lord."

THE NORMAL CHRISTIAN LIFE?

This is the way the Christian life ought to be. God is a person. He is not a stranger; He is our Father. Speaking to Him about the minor things in life and seeing tangible evidence of His loving response should be normal for Christians.

I do not believe that either one of that morning's instances was a coincidence. I do not believe I was lucky. I believe that a sovereign God was in control and personally interested in the DAWN movement, in GLINT, in the price of Christian books in the Philippines and in Rey Halili, Jim Montgomery, Georgalyn Wilkinson and Peter Wagner. That was one of those mornings I happened to be spiritually tuned in to what the Father was doing and it was a marvelous experience.

When I say this is the way the Christian life ought to be, I fully realize this is not the way it always is. Such mornings are infrequent enough so that after I talked to Georgalyn, I spent a few minutes taking notes on what had occurred. However, if I am accurately observing what is currently happening among Christian people in almost every part of the world these days, such mornings will become more and more frequent for people like you and me.

It could be that for some people, prayers concerning a speaking engagement or meeting a friend fall on the trivial end of the scale. Doesn't God have more important things to do?

Of course God has more important things on His agenda. But the glorious thing about God is that He has no such limits as we humans have. He can and does care for the trivial, while not in the least subtracting from caring for the matters that have a more universal impact. Such as, for example, the fall of the Iron Curtain.

PRAYER AND THE IRON CURTAIN

Since the disintegration of the Soviet Union in 1991, many stories of intense intercession have begun to surface, some on the part of believers within the USSR and some from believers without. One of my desires is that a creative, well-informed person will eventually compile these stories. It would provide us with what Paul Harvey might call, "The rest of the story."

One key piece of the puzzle has already been revealed. My friend Dick Eastman published the story in his classic work on intercession, *Love on Its Knees*, before the Iron Curtain came down. He tells of his friend Mark Geppert, whom God called in 1986 to spend two weeks in the Soviet Union and do nothing but pray. Mark reports that God gave him a specific itinerary and a prayer agenda before he went to the Soviet Union. His last assignment was to spend four days of prayer in Kiev, the closest major city to the small village of Chernobyl where the infamous nuclear reactor was located.

On the morning of the last day of his prayer journey, April 25, 1986, Mark went to the square in the center of Kiev and began to pray under a large statue of Lenin. He prayed in 15-minute segments, each marked by the chiming of the huge city clock on the square. During the 15-minute period just before noon, he felt the release. He sensed God saying that, in answer to prayer, something was then happening that would shake the Soviet Union and open the way for more freedom. In Mark's spirit God said, "Begin to praise Me for I have done it!" Mark did openly praise the King of kings right under the statue of Lenin. He then became bold enough to shake his fist at the statue and shout with feeling, "Lenin, you're history!"

In his elation, Mark dared to ask God for a confirmation. "Oh, God," he cried, "give me a sign, even a little sign." Just then the hands of the huge clock reached 12:00 noon. For four days the clock had chimed without fail on every hour. This time at 12:00 noon it was totally silent![1]

History now records that at 12:00 noon, or brief moments thereafter, the first mistake was made by a single worker at the Chernobyl nuclear power plant, which ultimately led to the disaster at about 1:30 A.M. on April 26, 1986, some 13 hours after God had released Mark Geppert.

"History Belongs to the Intercessors"

This incident was anything but trivial. Dick Eastman later shared with me a clipping from the *Washington Post* written five years after the Chernobyl event, arguing that the Chernobyl explosion "is increasingly seen as the culminating moment in the collapse of a political and economic system that was both cruel and hopelessly inefficient."[2]

Now the question whether this could have been a coincidence becomes more crucial than whether Peter Wagner meeting Georgalyn Wilkinson in Manila was a coincidence. Could it be that Mark Geppert's prayers (along with those of countless others) actually had something to do with the liberation of hundreds of millions of men and women from tyrannical political oppression? Could it be that prayer can make that much difference? Could Walter Wink be right when he says, "History belongs to the intercessors?"[3]

THE GREAT PRAYER MOVEMENT

More and more people in the nations around the world who have a significant Christian presence are answering yes to the above questions. A prayer movement that greatly surpasses anything like it in living memory, perhaps in all of Christian history, is rapidly gaining momentum. In all the years I have ministered to pastors across America, I have never seen prayer so high on their collective agendas.

The hunger for prayer knows no denominational boundaries. Evangelical, mainline, charismatic, Pentecostal, Episcopal, fundamentalist, Lutheran, Baptist, restorationist, Reformed, Mennonite, holiness, Calvinistic, dispensational, Wesleyan or you-name-it kinds of churches are surprising themselves at the growing interest in prayer. At clergy conferences, pastors are asking each other, still in somewhat guarded tones, "Is what we are seeing possibly the phenomenon that historians have been telling us usually precedes a true revival?" If so, they realize that it is not something being generated by hype or by extraordinary willpower, but by the Spirit of God.

Specialized prayer ministries are being organized across the country and around the world. Some come and go, others seem more stable, having boards of directors, regular funding and newsletters. The Christian community is currently benefiting from David Bryant's Concerts of Prayer, Gary Bergel's Intercessors for America, Leonard LeSourd's Breakthrough, Cindy Jacobs' Generals of Intercession, Esther Ilnisky's Esther Network International, Evelyn Christenson's United Prayer Ministries and Beth Alves's Intercessors International just to name a few. Some concentrate on personal intercession, some on praying for government, some for world evangelization, some on spiritual warfare, some on children.

Most such prayer ministries are interdenominational. But at the same time, the denominations themselves are recognizing the crucial importance of prayer and forming their own departments for denominational prayer ministries. Many, if not most, denominations in the United States now have prayer leaders on their staffs. The unlikely combination of denominational prayer leaders from the Christian Reformed Church, the Assemblies of God and the Southern Baptists met and prayed together not long ago and decided to form the Denominational Prayer Leaders Network. Alvin Vander Griend heads the steering committee and oversees their annual meeting.

The A.D. 2000 Movement

Currently, these worldwide denominational and independent prayer movements are being coordinated and synchronized by the A.D. 2000 and Beyond Movement. The focus of the movement is to catalyze the existing forces for evangelism all around the world for a massive evangelistic thrust during this decade. Its motto is, "A church for every people and the gospel for every person by A.D. 2000." Its key focal points are: (1) the 1,000 least evangelized cities of the world; (2) some 6,000 yet unreached people groups; and (3) the 10/40 Window—a geographical rectangle between 10 degrees and 40 degrees north latitude and running from North Africa on the west to Japan and the Philippines on the east. It is estimated that more than 90 percent of those in the unreached people groups live in or on the border of the 10/40 Window.

The A.D. 2000 Movement, directed by Luis Bush of Colorado Springs, Colorado, is the first international coordinating movement of its size to combine prayer with world evangelization on the highest level. A.D. 2000 is built on 10 semiautonomous tracks or resource networks, one of which is the United Prayer Track. My wife, Doris, and I have had the privilege of coordinating the United Prayer Track since its inception and it has put us in a strategic position to observe and evaluate the great, worldwide prayer movement. Wherever we go, we find prayer groups that want to be in touch with other prayer groups and together storm the heavenlies on behalf of those who are still in darkness.

For the first time in living memory, top-level Christian leaders of all stripes agree that the ultimate effectiveness of such essential activities as saturation church planting, penetrating the unevangelized cities—particularly on behalf of the poor—and reaching unreached peoples with cross-cultural missions, will rise or fall on the quantity and quality of the prayer ministry that precedes them and accompanies them. This is so biblical (e.g., Acts 4:24-30; Eph. 6:18-20; 2 Thess. 3:1), it seems strange to say that it is a new and different emphasis in high-level strategizing for world evangelization.

Prayer in the Liberal Camp

The prayer movement is not confined to evangelical churches. High-profile representatives of the more liberal, social-action camp, such as Walter Wink and Bill Wylie-Kellermann, are advocating prayer as the chief means to engage the powers that are corrupting society at all levels.

Speaking of the demise of the former Soviet Union, Walter Wink says, "We can believe that none of this would have happened without the demonstrations and prayers over the decades of the peace movement." He is not able to explain that the most vociferously anticommunist president of the United States, Ronald Reagan, negotiated the first nuclear reduction treaty with the USSR as anything but an answer to prayer. International political science per se could not have predicted it. Because of prayer, Wink says, "God found an opening, and was able to bring about a miraculous change of direction."[4]

As I have been writing on prayer over the past few years, I have found myself developing a growing sensitivity for many of the causes espoused by some of our liberal sisters and brothers. I say "many" because I must admit that some of the causes a few are supporting are so overtly contradictory to biblical morality that in my opinion they must be prayed *against* rather than prayed *for*. But peace between the United States and the former Soviet Union, freedom and human rights in Romania, food for famine victims in Africa or reconciliation of the races in America are not among those. They are clearly the will of the

Father, and evangelicals can fervently pray together with liberals, "Thy will be done on earth, as it is in heaven" (Matt. 6:10, *KJV*).

Those who have followed my writings know that in years past I have engaged in my share of polemics on evangelism versus social action. I think I can still make a sound biblical case for prioritizing evangelism in fulfilling our Kingdom responsibilities. Now, however, we seem to be discussing things on a higher plane. Rather than designing our ministries first of all on evangelistic techniques or political action we are mutually discovering that the real battle is a spiritual battle and that our primary action must be based on using spiritual, not carnal, weapons. From all camps, the consensus is that biblical prayer heads the list of spiritual weapons. More important than prioritizing evangelism over social action is prioritizing the spiritual over the technological.

Prayer is not a substitute for aggressive social action or persuasion evangelism. But the best strategies for either will be more effective with high quality prayer than without it.

This is not to imply in any way that prayer is a *substitute* for aggressive social action or persuasion evangelism. But it is to suggest that the best strategies for either will be more effective with high quality prayer than without it.

THE THREEFOLD CORD

In the first book in this *Prayer Warrior* series, *Warfare Prayer*, I told of the prophetic word I received in 1989 through Dick Mills concerning the "threefold cord" of Ecclesiastes 4:12. Through it, I understood that God would use me as a catalyst to help bring together three groupings of Christians He desired to use for His purposes of the 1990s: conservative evangelicals, charismatics and conscientious liberals. I went on to give many evidences in the book that the first two cords were indeed beginning to come together, but I did not deal specifically with the conscientious liberals.[5]

I was not clear then who these conscientious liberals might be, and I am still not totally clear. I have, however, advanced to the "something like" stage. I think they would be something like Walter Wink, whom I know personally and would describe to my evangelical friends as a born-again Christian who has a heart for serving God and who is open to the fulness and the ministry of the Holy Spirit.

Wink and I struggle with substantial disagreements on things, such as the identity of the supernatural principalities and powers and the positions we take on certain ethical issues. However, I agree with Walter when he says to me, "I trust you and I are in agreement that it is not so important that we settle our differences as that we agree to pray together, to fight for God's inbreaking new reality together....So I want to affirm my commitment to fighting on a common front with you against the Powers, however we conceive or misconceive them."[6]

We are beginning to see that if God's people are going to come together to implement His will in this decade, prayer will likely be the primary force to weave together the three cords.

UPSTREAMING TO KOREA

As new and exciting as the prayer movement seems to many of us, it is anything but new in Korea. The prayer movement began there in the first decade of our century and has continued building momentum ever since. I use the date 1970 as the time that the prayer movement began spilling over from Korea to the rest of the world. We Americans have been saying: "Someday we will not only send missionaries to the Third World but we will receive missionaries from the churches there and we will be enriched with what we learn from them." That day has now come. Along with many other examples of this, we and the rest of the world are learning much about prayer from our Korean friends.

Over the past 100 years, Protestant Christianity has grown from zero to more than 30 percent of the population of South Korea. At night in the city of Seoul, one can look across the urban landscape and see a half dozen neon red crosses marking churches along any given line of sight. Of the 20 churches in the world that count weekend attendance of 20,000 or more, 9 of them are in Korea alone. The largest Baptist church, the largest Methodist church, the largest Presbyterian church, the largest holiness church and the largest Pentecostal church in the world are all in Korea. David Yonggi Cho's Yoido Full Gospel Church is the world's largest, having a membership of 700,000.

How did this spectacular growth happen? Many have asked this question of Korean Christian leaders, and virtually all have received the same one-word answer: *prayer!*

Seoul hosted the Olympic Games in 1988. If there had been a gold medal for prayer, Korea would have won hands down. A special, open-air prayer meeting was called for the Olympics on August 15, 1988. One million Christians showed up to pray. But they had done it before. Another million-member prayer meeting had already been held as a National Day of Prayer the preceding October.

Korean Prayer Patterns

Many special prayer programs and events happen in Korea throughout the average year. But three strong patterns have emerged that are now being adapted in other nations as the great prayer movement advances.

1. Early-morning prayer. Early-morning prayer is as much a part of church life in Korea as is hearing sermons, singing hymns or taking up offerings in the churches most of us attend. No church in Korea is without an early-morning prayer meeting. Large churches and small churches, city churches and rural churches, rich churches and poor churches—all schedule prayer meetings in their sanctuary before the sun comes up 365 days a year.

While in Korea recently, I visited my good friend Pastor Sundo Kim of the Kwang Lim Methodist Church. This visit was toward the end of a special 40-day "Mount Horeb Prayer Meeting," during which he had called his congregation to special early-morning prayer. Even those who did not ordinarily attend the early-morning prayer meetings were urged to come each morning and pray from 5:00 to 6:00. He told me that attendance had been running between 3,000 and 4,000 each morning.

This I had to see. Pastor Kim agreed to provide transportation. The next morning his driver was to pick up Doris and me at our hotel; but it was not easy. A record-breaking storm engulfed Korea that night and more than 60 lives were lost to its fury. The rain and wind were so ferocious at 5:00 the next morning that I wondered if anyone at all would leave their homes for a prayer meeting. But the driver showed up, we went to the church and arrived after the meeting started; if someone had not reserved seats for us, we would not have had a place to sit. The 4,000-seat sanctuary was packed! What a prayer meeting!

On another recent visit to Korea, I had the privilege of attending the world's largest, early-morning prayer meeting at the Myong-Song Presbyterian Church, pastored by Kim Sam Hwan. The group I was with also had to call ahead for reserved seats at the 6:00 A.M. meeting, packed with 4,000 people. This, however, was the third such service that morning; others were held at 4:00 A.M. and 5:00 A.M. The usual, early-morning prayer meeting attendance at the Myong-Song Presbyterian Church is 12,000.

I began visiting Korea in the early 1970s, and attended predawn prayer meetings in a few of the churches. It soon became evident that a relatively small percentage of the church members habitually attended. I can remember consciously registering a mental assumption: In large churches, this activity is certainly one that the senior pastor would assign to other staff members. Wrong! I could not have been more mistaken. I was astonished to discover that these meetings were almost invariably led by the senior pastor.

This encouraged me to ask my senior-pastor friends why it was that they participated in each one of these early prayer meetings. They would first look at me with a puzzled expression as if to say, "Why such a stupid question?" Then, realizing that I was just another one of those American Christians, they would almost all give me an identical answer: "Because that's where the power is!" They had a full day of ministry ahead of them and they did not want to tackle it without God's power. They would have fully agreed with the title of Bill Hybels' excellent book: *Too Busy Not to Pray* (InterVarsity Press).

2. *Friday-night prayer meetings.* All-night prayer meetings are scheduled for Friday nights in almost all Korean churches. Typically, a substantial group of people will gather at 10:00 P.M. and pray together until dawn the next day.

In most of our Western churches, an all-night prayer meeting, if one is ever held, marks some special occasion. Attending one and hanging in to the end is looked upon as a rather extraordinary spiritual accomplishment. But Koreans take it in stride. This does not mean that every Korean Christian does it, but many of them do. It is common in the Yoido Full Gospel Church, for example, to have more than 10,000 people praying through the night. They are one of a growing number of churches that also schedule a Wednesday, all-night prayer meeting, and the attendance is similar. Given the fact that there are about 7,000 churches in Seoul, I would not doubt that on the average Friday night more than one-quarter-million Christians are praying all night in that one city alone.

3. Prayer mountains. At last count, more than 200 churches in Korea have purchased mountains on which they have built prayer retreat centers. Some are large, such as Pastor David Yonggi Cho's prayer mountain, where 3,000 people are always present and more than 10,000 on weekends. Some are luxurious, such as Pastor Sundo Kim's prayer mountain, which features an elegant, mile-long prayer garden. The garden includes 9 specially constructed prayer areas accommodating 30 to 200 pray-ers each, and is graced with life-size statues of Jesus and His disciples in various episodes of their ministry.

Many have prayer grottos carved into the sides of the mountain itself where a person can retreat to pray for hours or days. Some have no food service as it is assumed that fasting will accompany the prayers. At one prayer mountain I visited, the only food service was a medically designed diet for withdrawal from prolonged fasts. Twenty-one-day fasts are not uncommon. Forty-day fasts are also seen from time to time.

Prayer Closets
Korean pastors who have large enough churches to afford it

typically design two features into the pastor's study at the church, which I have found nowhere else.

One is a literal prayer closet with nothing but a pillow on the floor, a low stand for a Bible and perhaps a picture or two on the wall. They will spend a minimum of one hour a day, some more than that, praying in the closet with the door shut.

The second feature is a motel-type bedroom and bath attached to their study. Many of them routinely spend all of Saturday night in their church study, praying and fasting for God's blessing on the Sunday services.

No wonder so many American pastors and other Christian leaders who have visited Korea testify that their prayer life has never been the same. Larry Lea introduced many of these Korean practices to America when he pastored Church on the Rock in Texas. Many times I have heard my own executive pastor, Jerry Johnson of Lake Avenue Congregational Church of Pasadena, California, testify publicly that his spiritual life was revolutionized when he spent some days on a Korean prayer mountain.

A humorous anecdote came out of the Lausanne II Congress in Manila in 1989. At one point, the participants from the various nations were holding national meetings throughout the complex. I happened to run into one of the congress staff who had been assigned the responsibility of looking in on the meetings to see if they were functioning smoothly. I asked him what he found and he said:

- In the American meeting, the blacks were complaining about the whites.
- In the Japanese meeting, the evangelicals were complaining about the charismatics.
- In the German meeting, the theologians were complaining about each other.

- In the Korean meeting, the delegates were on their knees, praying together.

We all have so much to learn from the Koreans about prayer!

UNDERSTANDING EFFECTIVE PRAYER

All prayer is not equal.

The upsurge of the great prayer movement is surfacing some truths about prayer that are bringing a clearer understanding. For example, prayer is not just prayer. Some prayer is dull and boring, a routine to go through and get it over with. Other prayer is exciting, and it is exciting because it is effective.

What does the Scripture say about effective prayer?

One of the most quoted passages of Scripture on prayer comes from James 5:16: "The effective, fervent prayer of a righteous man avails much."

Some treat this Scripture casually as if it said that all prayer avails much. But closer examination shows that only a certain kind of prayer prayed by a certain kind of person is what avails much. If some prayer is *effective*, it follows that some prayer is also *ineffective*.

How can we tell the difference between effective prayer and ineffective prayer?

James 5:16 and 17 answer the question by using Elijah as the example of effective prayer. When Elijah prayed that it would not rain, it did not rain for $3^{1/2}$ years. Then when he prayed that it would rain, it rained. Effective prayer is prayer that is answered. Of course, sometimes the answers to our prayers are not as obvious or overt as other times.

Many kinds of prayer are used, all of which or none of which may be effective. I once carefully went through the book of Acts and found 23 instances of prayer. Depending on how one would cluster them, several varieties of prayer are modeled for us there. We have corporate prayer, group prayer and individual prayer. We have prayer of intercession and prayer of petition. We have prayer for physical healing, prayer for forgiveness, prayer of praise and thanksgiving. Prayer is used to commission people for ministry and to open them for the filling of the Holy Spirit. Some prayer is one-way, some is two-way.

How can we be sure that whatever kind of prayer we use is *effective* prayer?

Two of Jesus' statements in the Gospel of John give us some clear guidelines:

- Whatever you ask in My name, that I will do (John 14:13).
- If you abide in Me, and My words abide in you, you will ask what you desire, and it shall be done for you (John 15:7).

1. We ask in Jesus' name. The reason for this is that we by ourselves have no authority. Our authority is only a derived authority from Jesus. But if He gives us authority, we represent none less than the King of kings! This is the kind of authority a police officer has when directing traffic in a city or an ambassador has when representing the president in a foreign country. Without Jesus' authority, prayer cannot be effective.

2. We must abide in Jesus. When we abide in Jesus, first of all we become righteous. Not that we have any righteousness in ourselves, but that Jesus imparts to us His righteousness. The effective, fervent prayer of a *righteous* person avails much.

Equally important is that when we abide in Jesus we know the Father's will. When we pray, we then pray according to the will of the Father. This is what Elijah did. Notice that the story in 1 Kings 17 and 18 does not so much talk about Elijah "praying" as proclaiming what was known by him as the word and will of God (see 1 Kings 18:1,41-45). The only prayers that are answered are prayers according to the will of God. Intimacy with the Father is not only the key to effective prayer, it is the essence of prayer.

The only prayers that are answered are prayers according to the will of God. Intimacy with the Father is not only the key to effective prayer, it is the essence of prayer.

The combination of authority and intimacy makes our prayers effective. My wife, Doris, has served as my personal secretary for almost 30 years. When the telephone rings, the callers usually ask for me. She says, "He is not available now, but may I help you? I'm Mrs. Wagner." That makes all the difference in the world. Callers more than likely stay on the phone and their questions are answered. Doris makes decisions the average secretary could not make. First, she has the authority, which is communicated by the name. Second, she knows my will and acts accordingly. God expects us to do the same.

▬ REFLECTION QUESTIONS ▬

1. The chapter begins with testimonies of answered prayer, some on small things, some on large things. How is it that we can affirm that such things are answers to prayer instead of some natural coincidence?
2. Over the last few years, have you noticed an increased inter-

est in prayer among churches and Christian people? Try to recall and share some concrete examples from what you have seen or heard or read.

3. Some who have followed Peter Wagner's past writings will be surprised at the things he says about prayer as a common ground with many liberals. Do you think he may be going too far in this direction?

4. Review the examples of the outstanding prayer life of Korean Christians. Which of these do you think could be successfully introduced into the churches of your city?

5. If it is true that not all prayer is effective, could you think of some specific examples of *ineffective* prayer that you or people you know have tried? How could this have been more effective?

Notes
1. The information for this case study is taken from Dick Eastman, *Love on Its Knees* (Grand Rapids, MI: Chosen Books, 1989), pp. 13-17; a pamphlet by Dick Eastman, "A Promise to Moscow" and personal conversations with Eastman.
2. Michael Dobbs, article in *Washington Post*, April 26, 1991.
3. Walter Wink, *Engaging the Powers* (Minneapolis, MN: Fortress Press, 1992), p. 298.
4. Ibid., p. 310.
5. C. Peter Wagner, *Warfare Prayer* (Ventura, CA: Regal Books, 1992), pp. 40,41.
6. Walter Wink, "Demons and DMins: The Church's Response to the Demonic," *Review Expositor* (Vol. 89, No. 4, Fall 1992), p. 512.

Rhetoric Prayer Versus Action Prayer

O

I AM VERY MUCH INTERESTED IN THE RELATIONSHIP BETWEEN prayer and church growth. For more than 20 years, I have been a professor of church growth at Fuller Seminary, and the last 5 of those years have been dedicated to research on prayer. I have spoken to many pastors across the country about this and some patterns have now become clear.

One of them is the difference between what I have come to call "rhetoric prayer" and "action prayer."

PRAYER AND CHURCH GROWTH

I think that what I am going to say is accurate, although I admit I do not have much statistical research to back it up. Nevertheless, suppose I selected a sample of 100 pastors of growing churches. Suppose I asked each one of them this question: In your experience, what role has prayer played in the growth of your church?

I am reasonably sure that virtually every one of them would respond, "Oh, prayer has played a central role in our growth."

I am also reasonably sure that for some 95 out of the 100 pastors such a response would be nothing but rhetoric. By that I do not mean that the pastors did not believe in prayer or that they in any sense intended to give a deceptive answer. But I do mean that if a careful study were made of the prayer life of their churches, I would not be surprised if little or no difference were found between them and the prayer life of the nongrowing churches in their same community.

Could I be wrong? Of course. I even *hope* that I am wrong. Knowing the power of prayer, I anticipated that I would find a strong correlation between quantity and quality of prayer and rates of church growth. Not that the correlation is totally absent. Research by C. Kirk Hadaway suggests that increased prayer has accompanied growth in some Southern Baptist churches.[1] That is why I allowed for a hypothetical 5 churches out of 100 that might truly be able to show a correlation between their prayer life and the growth of the church. I will give some illustrations of this in due time. But across the board, I am afraid that my observation is correct.

The "Ought" and the "Is"

Let me reinforce my point with a bit of irony. To my knowledge, the one person who has taken the lead in seriously attempting to research this issue is Terry Teykl, pastor of the Aldersgate United Methodist Church in College Station, Texas. His book, *Pray and Grow*[2] is the only book I know of that deals with the relationship of prayer to church growth. This is just the beginning of Teykl's research and the statistical part I referred to above has not yet been done. Needless to say, Teykl agrees with me that we *should* find a correlation, and writes his book on that premise.

But what about these hypothetical pastors? Apparently, if

we do not prime the pump by asking them directly what role prayer plays in the growth of their churches, chances are they won't mention it. This is affirmed in the foreword to Terry Teykl's book, written by Ezra Earl Jones of the United Methodist General Board of Discipleship, an agency closely in touch with Methodist pastors across the nation.

Ezra Earl Jones cites some research, which in fact has been done. They selected growing Methodist churches and asked the pastors of those churches to rank, in order, the 10 top factors contributing to their growth. Here they are, in order: vital worship services, fellowship, the pastor, sharply targeted ministries, community and world outreach, Christian education, planning for church growth, physical facilities and location, lay ministries and evangelistic outreach. *Not a single one of the 10 is prayer!*

Of course, these pastors may have felt that it was inappropriate to mention prayer, but the irony is that the foreword in a book arguing that prayer *ought* to be a strong growth factor produces evidence that it *isn't.* At least it isn't something that pastors of growing churches would verbalize as being important.

What Does the Rhetoric Mean?

I hope it is clear that I am not criticizing these Methodist pastors. I am simply trying to provide an accurate description of the actual situation among many American churches. What do pastors of growing churches mean when they say that prayer is a key to their growth, although they would not include it in the list of the top 10 factors?

I am sure they mean:

- The power of God is behind our growth. Jesus said, "I will build My church" (Matt. 16:18). Paul said, "I planted, Apollos watered, but God gave the increase"

(1 Cor. 3:6). Our church is growing, not primarily because of human effort, but by God's blessing.

- I preach on prayer frequently. Not that I have given many entire sermons over to prayer, but I often mention prayer and teach my people that prayer is extremely important for our personal lives and the life of the church.
- I regularly pray for the church and its life and growth. Many others in the congregation also pray frequently for our church.

Although the above statements are true and commendable, if the week-in and week-out prayer life of such churches were rated on a scale of 1 to 10, they would be pretty low, even if the ranking were done by the pastors themselves.

I do not know how many times I have heard pastors say, "The Wednesday evening prayer meeting is the most important meeting of the week in our church." But, with rare exceptions, it is not that at all. It is the dullest, least attended, most routine and most boring meeting of the week. In most cases, the church would grow at the same rate with or without the Wednesday evening prayer meeting.

The honest conclusion is that most growing churches, at least in America, are growing because of the conscious or unconscious application of sound church growth principles accompanied by a fairly low level of prayer. I have yet to find a church that did not believe in prayer and practice it at least to some extent. However, I agree with Terry Teykl. I believe that the growth of these churches would be much more dynamic if it were accompanied by a *high level* of prayer. They now are like eight-cylinder cars running on four or five cylinders.

In this book, I want to encourage pastors to make the transition from *rhetoric prayer* to *action prayer.*

I believe action prayer can:

- Help growing churches increase their growth rate and deepen the spiritual quality of their churches.
- Turn around nongrowing churches.
- Change the spiritual atmosphere over the community as a whole for more social justice and evangelistic openness.

From Rhetoric to Action

I consider myself an expert of sorts on rhetoric prayer. I practiced it rather consistently for the first 25 years of my career as an ordained minister. After several years of transition, I am now trying to practice action prayer. The last 5 years of my ministry have by far been the most exciting and rewarding years of all. Action prayer has made the difference.

As I analyze the transition from rhetoric prayer to action prayer, I would point to at least three areas on which churches and church leaders would do well to concentrate. Undoubtedly there are many more than three, but these seem to me to

---

The most helpful way to understand action prayer is to realize it is basically a relationship. Through prayer we abide in God. Prayer draws us into intimacy with the Father. It is a personal relationship.

---

be of supreme importance. The three areas are: (1) understanding the nature of prayer; (2) recognizing the power of prayer; and (3) following the rules of prayer.

UNDERSTANDING THE NATURE OF PRAYER

Generally, people think of prayer as asking God for something. But this is only a part of what praying is; it does not accurately describe the *essence* of prayer. The most helpful way to understand action prayer is to realize it is basically a relationship. Through prayer we abide in God. Prayer draws us into intimacy with the Father. It is a personal relationship.

When Jesus taught His disciples to pray, He told them to begin, "Our Father who art in heaven" (Matt. 6:9, *NASB*). This is a declaration of not only a relationship, but a family-type relationship. The most awesome thing about prayer is that it brings us into the presence of God, not as though we were sitting in a stadium and looking at the figure of God down there on the platform, but as though we were sitting together in our living room.

Prayer Pleases God

The book of Revelation speaks of prayer only twice, and both times prayer is described as incense. In Revelation 5, we are looking at the majestic, throne-room scene where Jesus takes a scroll sealed with seven seals from the Father. Twenty-four elders fall down to worship and each has "golden bowls full of incense, which are the prayers of the saints" (Rev. 5:8). Then again in Revelation 8, an angel appears at the altar to offer incense along with the prayers of all the saints. "And the smoke of the incense, with the prayers of the saints, ascended before God from the angel's hand" (Rev. 8:4).

As the apostle John writes this in Revelation, he is certainly familiar with Psalm 141:2: "Let my prayer be set before You as incense, the lifting up of my hands as the evening sacrifice." This was a reference to the altar of incense in the Tabernacle. Aaron, the priest, burned incense there every morning and every night to symbolize the day-by-day relationship between God and His people.

Thanks to Jesus Christ and His death on the cross, we do not have to depend on a priest such as Aaron to burn incense to remind us of our relationship to God. Our prayers are in themselves that relationship. And each one of us can go directly to God.

God enjoys this prayer relationship. He likes the atmosphere produced by the incense. It almost seems arrogant to say it, but God is blessed by our prayers. Because of Jesus we have the overwhelming privilege of a Father-child relationship with none less than the Creator of the universe. We sit with Him in our living room.

Action Prayer Is Two-Way

Although some might not have thought of defining prayer as intimacy with the Father, few who read this will disagree. But there is an implication that goes along with understanding prayer as intimacy that many do not consciously accept. If prayer is a relationship, the relationship must be two-way, not just one-way.

The New Testament instructs us to relate to God as our Father and assumes we will know how to do this by what we have learned through our human relationships. At this writing, my father is 87 and lives more than 3,000 miles away. We love each other and have always had a very good relationship. I dedicated this book to him. We maintain our relationship by a functional substitute for prayer—the telephone. I call him at least once a week, but when I do we both talk. Not once have I expected that I would do all the talking.

However, through my own years of rhetoric prayer, that is more or less the extent of what I was expecting with my heavenly Father; it was one-way. I talked to Him and never listened for a response. Oh, I looked for answers to my prayers, mainly through rearranged circumstances of my life. But hearing His voice? I knew that John said, "That which we have seen and heard we declare to you, that you also may have fellowship with us; and truly our fellowship is with the Father and with His Son Jesus Christ" (1 John 1:3), but I never drew the conclusion that as part of our fellowship, God desired a two-way conversation.

Hearing the voice of God is so important for action prayer that I am going to deal with it in some depth in the next chapter.

RECOGNIZING THE POWER OF PRAYER

For rhetoric prayer to become action prayer, it is essential to recognize a very simple truth: *Prayer works!*

By that, I mean that when we pray correctly we see answers to prayer. The answers do not always take the form we expect, but they frequently do. The answers do not always come at the time we expect them, but they frequently do. Sometimes the answers are partial, but frequently they not only meet our expectations, they exceed them.

God is known "to do exceedingly abundantly above all that we ask or think" (Eph. 3:20).

I fully realize that many who are reading this are already action pray-ers and they need no convincing that prayer works. It is hard for some to believe that in our evangelical Christian world today there are those who would discourage us from asking God for something in prayer with the expectation that, in response, God will grant it. But there are.

Should Answers to Prayer Excite Us?

I usually avoid polemics, and I will continue to do so here by disguising names and places. But I think this issue is absolutely crucial to full participation in the great prayer movement of our day, and therefore I am going to clarify the issue as sharply as I can. In order to identify it, I will say that I am citing an official editorial in a prominent, conservative, evangelical periodical, written and published within the last five years.

The background for the editorial was a fairly widespread, publicized experiment in prayer by cardiologist Randolph C. Byrd of San Francisco General Hospital. I referred to the study in my book *How to Have a Healing Ministry* (Regal Books). Byrd divided 400 heart patients randomly into 2 groups of 200 each. No one else, neither the patients nor the medical personnel, knew who was in which group. One group was prayed for by born-again Christians and the other group was not prayed for. The group that was prayed for developed significantly fewer complications and fewer of them died.

Most Christians I know would rejoice at this finding. But this particular editor felt that he should warn his readers about a danger lurking behind such evidence. He contends, for example, that we should not use this kind of evidence to teach our children to pray. If we do, they can miss the more important lesson: obedience. "We pray first to obey," he argues, "not to profit."

Neither, he suggests, should we use it to convince our friends to pray more. If we do, and if later on some prayer is not answered, prayer in general can lose its appeal. He thinks that sharing good news about answered prayer is like giving our kids treats. It might taste good at the time, "But a steady diet of candy is not what good nutrition is all about."

The editor summarizes his position by saying, "Reducing prayer to a technique for self-gratification will make our theology sick."

Perpetuating Rhetoric Prayer

The notion that we are theologically healthier if we do not expect our prayers to be answered is alive and well. Nothing I am aware of contributes more to perpetuating rhetoric prayer. I was programmed in this way of thinking in my own training for the ministry, but I doubt that any of my professors were quite that outspoken. I wonder what the editor's response would have been if his wife, for example, had been one of those heart patients who received prayer.

A recent study by Margaret Poloma and George Gallup, Jr. found that although 88 percent of Americans pray to God in some way or other, less than half of them (42 percent) ask Him for material things they might need. And only 15 percent regularly experience receiving answers to specific prayer requests.[3] One of the reasons so few practice "petitionary prayer" may well be that the theology of our editor friend has been carrying the day, including evangelicals.

Poloma and Gallup found that "many who ask do receive that for which they have prayed." Their comment: "A modern and rational worldview may regard petitionary prayer as a form of magic, but it is a prayer form for which there are countless biblical examples."[4]

I would add that a primary biblical example of praying for material things is the Lord's Prayer itself in which Jesus instructed us to pray, "Give us this day our daily bread" (Matt. 6:11).

The Sovereignty of God and the Law of Prayer

As I recall, I was taught in seminary that the most important function of prayer was to change me and mold me. God never changes. He is sovereign and He will do what He intends to do whether I pray or not. A saintly voice from yesteryear, that of R. A. Torrey, sounds as if it were speaking today. Torrey laments that churches in his day were not praying. Christians, he says, "believe in prayer as having a beneficial 'reflex influence,' that is, as benefiting the person who prays...but as for prayer bringing anything to pass that would not have come to pass if we had not prayed, they do not believe in it, and many of them frankly say so."[5] Rhetoric prayer was common then as well.

Fortunately, attitudes toward prayer are changing rapidly in our day. The great prayer movement would not be sweeping the globe if prayer did not work. Advocates of action prayer in no way question the sovereignty of God. But they understand from Scripture that the sovereign God has established a law of prayer. God *desires to do* many things, but He *will not do* them unless or until Christian people, using their God-given freedom, pray and ask Him to do it (see Jas. 4:2). And such prayer does not *violate* our obedience to God; just the opposite. It is *done* in obedience to God (see Matt. 6:8; 7:7-11; Luke 11:9-13).

No one can change God, but our prayers can have a direct influence on what God does or does not do. This is the way God Himself has structured reality. "Call to Me, and I will answer you, and show you great and mighty things, which you do not know" (Jer. 33:3). Suppose we do not call on Him? The answer is too obvious to state.

When I pray, I am not telling God what to do; He could do nothing against His will. I am praying that whatever He wants to do will in fact be done. My presumption is that if I do not pray, something that God Himself desires will, in fact, not be done. I love the title of a chapter in Jack Hayford's popular book, *Prayer Is Invading the Impossible* (Ballantine Books): "If We Don't, He Won't."

No group holds the sovereignty of God in higher esteem than Calvinists. That is why I think my friend Alvin Vander Griend's opinion on this matter is so important. Alvin comes from the Christian Reformed denomination, which has named its theological seminary for John Calvin. Vander Griend says:

> God waits to be asked not because He is powerless but because of the way He has chosen to exercise His will. We are not pawns on a giant chessboard. We are involved. Only a cold, hard, mechanistic view of God's sovereignty and predestination assumes that God discounts our prayer and simply moves in accord with a predetermined once-for-all plan. This is not a biblical

view of God; it more resembles a fatalistic, Muslim-like view of sovereignty that the Bible repudiates.[6]

Prayer Changes History

No one has said it better than Richard Foster in his classic, *Celebration of Discipline:* "We are working with God to determine the future. Certain things will happen in history if we pray rightly."[7]

One of the books on prayer I currently recommend to my students at Fuller Seminary has a provocative title: *And God Changed His Mind.* It is written by Brother Andrew, who says, "God's plans for us are not chiseled in concrete. Only His character and nature are unchanging; His decisions are not!"[8]

The Bible gives several examples of God changing His plans because of intercession. One was His intention to pour out His wrath and consume Israel when Moses came back from Sinai with the tablets of the Law. But Moses interceded on the Israelites' behalf. "So the Lord relented from the harm which He said He would do to His people" (Exod. 32:14).

It is important for us to realize that all that happens in this world is not the will of God. It is not a pleasant thought, but Satan is described as no less than "the god of this age" (2 Cor. 4:4). It is God's will, for example, that none should perish (see 2 Pet. 3:9), but many do because the god of this age has blinded their minds (see 2 Cor. 4:3,4).

We are told in Scripture that Daniel prayed and God answered his prayer on the same day. However, the answer took 21 days to arrive, not because God was slow, but because the "Prince of Persia" succeeded in delaying it (see Dan. 10). In addressing this, Walter Wink suggests, "This new element in prayer—the resistance of the Powers to God's will—marks a decisive break with the notion that God is the cause of all that happens."[9] If Daniel had not continued fasting and praying, would the answer have *ever* arrived? Probably not. That is why prayer is so important and why history belongs to the intercessors, as Wink would say.

The Christian Life Center

Pastor Waymon Rodgers founded the Christian Life Center in Louisville, Kentucky, in the early 1980s. The Center grew well up to 500, but then took a nosedive and went back down to 200. Rodgers became discouraged and began to look for another church. Then a word came from God: "I've called you to Louisville, and I'll give you the keys to the city."

The key turned out to be prayer. Rodgers, who is now with the Lord, challenged 7 deacons to pray with him 1 hour each day. He presented the need to the congregation and 100 of the 200 agreed to pray regularly for the church. He started praying and maintained a 22-hour-a-day prayer chain. The church stepped out in faith and purchased 346 acres to install a Korean-type prayer mountain complete with prayer grottos, motel-type rooms and a chapel. They designated every Thursday as a day of prayer and fasting.

In the Christian Life Center, prayer was not simply rhetoric, it was lively action. The church turned around almost instantly. It grew to 2,000, then to 6,000. By then it had become the center from which 55 new churches had been planted in the state.

Prayer is powerful. It works!

FOLLOWING THE RULES OF PRAYER

I have lost count of how many books on prayer I have read in the past few years. One of the striking things is that hardly any two of the books are the same. Prayer is probably an inexhaustible subject. Many "rules of prayer" are in existence, but I want to highlight the four that those of us who have been practicing rhetoric prayer need to pay special attention to if we desire to shift into action prayer.

The four rules of prayer I feel are the most crucial include:

- Praying with faith;
- Praying with a pure heart;
- Praying with power;
- Praying with persistence.

RULE 1: PRAYING WITH FAITH

James tells us that if we lack wisdom we should ask God for it (see Jas. 1:5). Then he adds, "But let him ask in faith, with no doubting, for he who doubts is like a wave of the sea driven and tossed by the wind" (Jas. 1:6). How important is this? James says it makes all the difference. The doubter must not "suppose that he will receive anything from the Lord" (Jas. 1:7). Faith clearly is an important rule of prayer.

Jesus taught His disciples about faith by using a graphic example: With faith they could tell a mountain to be cast into the sea and it would happen (see Mark 11:23). Then He said, "Whatever things you ask when you pray, believe that you will receive them, and you will have them" (Mark 11:24).

What is faith? "Faith is the substance of things hoped for, the evidence of things not seen" (Heb. 11:1). Naturally, we do not ask God for something we already have but for something that we do not as yet have. We hope for it. We do not see it. But if we have faith, the unseen things we hope for will have substance. This substance cannot be material, it must be spiritual, but it is substance nonetheless. If we do not give substance to the things we pray for, we will be doubters like the waves of the sea and our prayers will go unanswered. We will have violated a rule of prayer.

Many do not like this teaching. They feel it is dangerous because it gives us too much responsibility. They do not like to face the fact that sometimes (certainly not all of the time) we ourselves are to blame for our prayers not being answered. Action prayer requires faith. Does God ever allow exceptions to this rule? Fortunately, for most of us, including me, He does. But let's be clear—they are the exceptions, not the rule.

Prosperity Theology

For years now, I have listened to criticisms of the "Word of Faith" or "prosperity theology" camp. But as I see it, their best advocates are simply trying to bring balance to the church by emphasizing a biblical truth that many of us have tended to ignore, namely, the crucial role that our human faith has in seeing God's will done.

I have also listened to criticisms of the practice of "visualization." When I first heard about visualization from close friends such as David Yonggi Cho and Robert Schuller, I could only recognize that these people knew something I did not know. They helped me to understand what Hebrews 11:1 meant by "substance," and I was grateful.

Have some of the Word of Faith people or the visualization people gone too far? Undoubtedly they have, but this is to be expected when a major midcourse correction comes into the Body of Christ. Have some Presbyterians gone too far with predestination? Have some Church of Christ people gone too far with baptismal regeneration? Have some Nazarenes gone too far with holiness? Have some Assemblies of God people gone too far with speaking in tongues? Have some Lutherans gone too far with law and gospel? Of course.

Balance will come. Some in the prosperity camp have already admitted that they have exaggerated the role of faith in answered prayer. Some have realized that there was a danger of feeling they could manipulate God; they know they should not do that. Some have recognized that the line between God-given prosperity and outright greed was somewhat blurred. Some have confessed that they have asked and not received because they asked amiss to "spend it on your pleasures" (Jas. 4:3).

Given the risks, we must nevertheless agree that praying with faith is a cardinal rule of prayer. Answers will come or be withheld on that basis.

How can we pray with more faith?

The major key to praying with faith is knowing the will of God. John tells us, "If we ask anything according to His will, He hears us" (1 John 5:14).

The Big "If"

Some people have not known how to handle praying with faith and their prayer life has suffered as a result. They have been so worried about the dangers of presumption and manipulating God that they have developed a fail-safe method of praying. They have discovered that when they prudently introduce the word "if" into strategic points of their prayer they do not need to be concerned whether their prayers are answered or not.

In his book *The Power of Positive Praying*, John Bisagno titled a chapter "If It Be Thy Will." He writes, "Many wonderful prayers have gone unanswered because they were rendered powerless with the word 'if' in the middle of them." Why do people do this? Bisagno suggests that the real reason behind this is: "We do not really believe that God is going to do anything so we have an easy way out in case He doesn't—an escape clause in fine print."[10] In other words, many people do not have biblical faith.

John Calvin would agree with Bisagno. In his *Institutes of the Christian Religion*, Calvin asks what sort of a prayer something like this would be: "O Lord, I am in doubt whether thou willist to hear me, but because I am pressed by anxiety, I flee to thee, that, if I am worthy, thou mayest help me." Calvin asserts that the prayers of the saints in the Scriptures do not follow this pattern. He admonishes us to follow the Holy Spirit's instructions to "come boldly to the throne of grace" (Heb. 4:16). John Calvin says, "Only that prayer is acceptable to God which is born, if I may so express it, out of such presumption of faith, and is grounded in unshaken assurance of hope."[11]

There is often a subtle assumption behind the phrase, "If it be thy will." The assumption is that it is not possible to know God's will before we pray. Some cite James 4:15: "You ought to say, 'If the Lord wills, we shall live and do this or that,'" to justify the assumption, perhaps without noticing that the context is planning a business trip, not addressing the Father in prayer.

Knowing the Will of God

But can we know the will of God before we pray?

Certainly. Two major ways to know the will of God are: (1) reading it in Scripture (see 2 Tim. 3:15,16); and (2) asking Him and getting a response (see John 14:26; 16:13; 2 Tim. 2:7; Jas. 1:5-7).

Most of what we need to know about God's will is revealed to us in the Bible. We know God's will concerning feeding the hungry, extramarital sex, justice for the oppressed, paying our taxes, obeying our parents and harmony of the races. The Bible is clear on these things, so when we pray for them we know we are praying God's will.

It is becoming popular in some circles to spend a good proportion of prayer time in *Praying the Scriptures,* to use the title of an excellent book on the subject by Judson Cornwall. In his book, Cornwall suggests that the biblical text can become the prayer we pray. He says, "When used as the vehicle of our prayers, the Word of God is capable of declaring deep inner desires and thoughts of the soul-spirit."[12] When we use the words of Scripture for our prayers we will be praying the will of God.

The second way of praying according to God's will is to ask Him and determine His will before we pray. Jesus said that He only did what He saw the Father doing (see John 5:19). We are to do likewise.

A major key to knowing the Father's will is to spend time with Him. Can we know the will of our spouse? After more than 40 years of living with my wife, I had better know her will, and I do. And she knows mine. Neither one of us knew on our wedding day what we know now. But we learned and we soon discovered that the quicker we learned the happier we were. The same applies to our heavenly Father. The more time we spend with Him, the surer we become of what is and is not His will.

How we can hear from Him while we are spending time with Him will be detailed in the next chapter.

When we do know God's will, whether through Scripture or through direct communication with God, we can then pray with all the faith expected of us and see corresponding answers to our prayers.

RULE 2: PRAYING WITH A PURE HEART

Recalling that the essence of prayer is an intimate relationship with the Father, it becomes obvious that any sin that obstructs that relationship, even partially, will reduce the effectiveness of our prayers.

Isaiah affirms God's desire to hear and respond to our prayers: "Behold, the Lord's hand is not shortened, that it cannot save; nor His ear heavy, that it cannot hear" (Isa. 59:1). Sin, however, can prevent it from happening. "But your iniquities have separated you from your God; and your sins have hidden His face from you, so that He will not hear" (Isa. 59:2). Dealing with sin and having a pure heart is an established rule of prayer.

Jesus recognizes this when, in the Lord's Prayer, He instructs us to pray daily: "Forgive us our sins" (Matt. 6:12, *TLB*). (The more common words "debts" or "trespasses" are obsolete and they mask today's real meaning of this prayer.) Because all Christians sin from time to time, we need to make sure the slate is clean daily if we expect our prayers to be answered. Peter reminds us, "The eyes of the Lord are on the righteous, and his ears are open to their prayers; but the face of the Lord is against those who do evil" (1 Pet. 3:12).

Repentance and confession of sin are essential for good praying. So is not sinning in the future, and that is why Jesus has us pray, "Lead us not into temptation" (Matt. 6:13, *NIV*). These contribute greatly to purifying the heart. But it seems that of all the sins we need to deal with to pray well, one stands out over the others: *forgiveness*.

Forgiving Others
The second part of "Forgive us our sins" is, "as we have forgiven those who have sinned against us" (Matt. 6:12, *TLB*). The reason I say forgiveness stands out above the other sins for good praying is that this is the only part of the Lord's prayer that Jesus underscores immediately after giving it. He says, "For if you forgive men their trespasses, your heavenly Father will also forgive you. But if you do not forgive men their trespasses, neither will your Father forgive your trespasses" (Matt. 6:14,15).

Suppose you have been really wronged? Suppose you are a bona fide victim? Suppose none of the fault was yours, but you were severely wounded by that other person? Suppose they refuse to say they are sorry? Suppose they tell others it was all your fault? What should you do?

Forgive them! Jesus did.

If you do forgive, it will purify your heart. The answers to your prayers do not depend on what your adversary does or does not do. They depend on what *you* do.

James 4 deals with prayers that are not answered because of

violating the pure heart rule. "You ask and do not receive" (Jas. 4:3). Why?

- You have wrong desires. You lust and you fight and you covet (see Jas. 4:2).
- You have wrong motives. You ask amiss. You do not ask according to God's will so you are off track (see Jas. 4:3).
- You have wrong objectives. You ask to satisfy your own pleasures. You are selfish (see Jas. 4:3).

The fruit of the Holy Spirit in our lives will refocus the way we come to God. The Holy Spirit will give us: (1) the right desire—intimacy with the Father; (2) the right motive—to glorify God; and (3) the right objective—to do God's will. This will help bring us into line, using the rule of praying with a pure heart.

RULE 3: PRAYING WITH POWER

One of the reasons we tend to lack faith in our praying is that we do not fully realize how much power we have when we come to the Father in Jesus' name. A rule of prayer we must follow is to utilize the power that has already been granted to us.

The difference between powerful prayer and weak prayer is the Holy Spirit. The Holy Spirit was the source of Jesus' miraculous power (see Matt. 12:28; Luke 4:1,14-18; Acts 2:22; 10:38), and Jesus told His disciples that they would have the same power and that they would do the works He did (see John 14:12). Before He left earth, Jesus told His disciples it was to their advantage that He was going because only then would they receive the full power of the Holy Spirit (see John 16:7-14). He instructed them to tarry in Jerusalem until they received this power (see Luke 24:49). Then just before Jesus went to heaven He said, "But you shall receive power when the Holy Spirit has come upon you" (Acts 1:8).

Although every born-again Christian enjoys the presence of the Holy Spirit in his or her life, not all enjoy it in the same measure. Some are filled with the Holy Spirit at any given time and some are not. I may be filled with the Holy Spirit today, but tomorrow I will need to renew my relationship with Him (see Eph. 5:18). Some call it baptism rather than filling. Different groups give it different doctrinal and practical embellishments. But the phenomenon is the same: although we all have the generic presence of the Holy Spirit, the quantity of the Holy Spirit's power can vary (see 1 Tim. 4:14; 2 Tim. 1:6).

Peter was one of those who was "filled with the Holy Spirit" (Acts 2:4) on the day of Pentecost. Nevertheless, Peter was "filled with the Holy Spirit" again in Acts 4:8 for his ministry to the Sanhedrin. Once, apparently, was not enough.

Our constant, day-by-day renewal of the presence of the Holy Spirit helps us in the other aspects of prayer. He helps us to maintain a pure heart because one of the works of the Holy Spirit is to convict us of sin (see John 16:8). He helps us be sure that we know the will of God as we enter into prayer because He draws us to the Father (see Rom. 8:16; Gal. 4:6). He builds our faith because we are encouraged by seeing supernatural power flowing through us and touching others.

When we have the Holy Spirit, we can truly pray with power.

RULE 4: PRAYING WITH PERSISTENCE

I mentioned earlier that sometimes the answers to our prayers do not come as rapidly as we hope they will. When this happens, we should continue to pray. Daniel, as we have seen, prayed 21 days before the answer to his prayer arrived (see

Dan. 10:12,13). He demonstrated for us the rule of praying with persistence.

Jesus said, "Men always ought to pray and not lose heart" (Luke 18:1), and then went on to illustrate it with the parable of the widow and the unjust judge. Although the judge himself did not intend to deal with the widow's case, he finally changed his mind because of her persistence. This was a nasty judge, but persistence paid off. But God is not nasty; He is good. If persistence was appropriate in the worst-case scenario, how much more will it be with a God disposed toward love and compassion.

Obviously, persistence could be overdone. I believe that if we have faith and a pure heart, our pattern should be to continue to pray until one of three things happens.

Stop praying when you see the answer. This is the most obvious of the three.

I recall during a break at a conference I was doing in Texas, a man came up to me and he was obviously having difficulty breathing. He knew it was a critical asthma attack that could be life-threatening. Soon after I began praying for him he coughed loudly and strongly, a mysterious white cloud came out of his mouth and evaporated into the atmosphere, and he began to breathe normally.

I mention this because it was one of those times when I could actually see the answer to my prayer. So I stopped praying, praised the Lord together with him, and he was fine for the rest of the conference. I never prayed for him again.

Stop praying when the Holy Spirit gives you confidence that the spiritual battle is won. A pastor from Zambia who had been studying at Fuller Seminary for a time had finally made arrangements to bring his wife and five children to the United States. At the beginning of a two-week course, he asked us to pray that his family would get reserved airplane seats, otherwise they would have to fly standby. And it would be difficult to find six empty seats.

The first day we prayed, the pastor's family did not get airplane seats. But we persisted and prayed every day that first week. Twice more his wife was refused seats. On Monday of the second week, I kindly suggested that we continue praying for her. But the pastor said we must not pray. God had told him over the weekend that He had answered our prayers, and he felt that if we continued to pray it would show lack of faith in the assurance God had given him. He said it was time to switch from faith to hope.

This sort of experience was new to me, but not to the Zambian pastor. Africans may know things that Americans do not know. I followed his suggestion, and God was faithful. The family came on the next airplane!

As Christian people tune in more accurately to the nature of prayer, as they move in the power of prayer and as they adhere to the rules of prayer, we will see many of our churches turned around and our communities opened to the gospel.

Stop praying when God says no. The apostle Paul wanted to get rid of his thorn in the flesh, whatever that might have been. He was persistent enough to ask the Lord three times to take it away. In this case God said no and, although He does not always do this, He gave Paul the reason. God said Paul needed the thorn in the flesh "lest I be exalted above measure" (2 Cor. 12:7).

Of course, there is no principle in praying only 3 times as Paul did in this case. God may want us to pray 30 times or 300 times. I think our human tendency is to conclude that the answer is no before it really is. I almost made that mistake in praying for the salvation of my father and mother. It was after 42 years of persistence (spotty at times, I must confess) that they gave their lives to Jesus Christ.

Our rhetoric prayer *can* become action prayer, and I am seeing this happen in churches across the United States and in other parts of the world. As Christian people tune in more accurately to the nature of prayer, as they move in the power of prayer and as they adhere to the rules of prayer, we will see many of our churches turned around and our communities opened to the gospel.

■ REFLECTION QUESTIONS ■

1. Why is it that many pastors will say that prayer is the most important activity of their church when, in fact, it is not?

2. If we agree that the true essence of prayer is intimacy with the Father, what are some of the concrete applications that will have to be made in our personal prayer lives?

3. Some feel that we should share tangible answers to prayer with enthusiasm, others advocate a more modest and restrained attitude toward desiring explicit answers. Discuss the pros and cons of each side.

4. In what sense does prayer cause God to "change His mind" as one author puts it? What is it about God that no human initiative changes?

5. "If it be your will" is frequently a part of our prayers. List

some instances where this is appropriate and then list some where it may not be appropriate.

Notes

1. C. Kirk Hadaway, *Church Growth Principles*, (Nashville, TN: Broadman Press, 1991), p. 51.
2. Terry Teykl, *Pray and Grow* (Discipleship Resources, P.O. Box 189, Nashville, TN 37202, 1988).
3. Margaret M. Poloma and George H. Gallup, Jr., *Varieties of Prayer* (Philadelphia, PA: Trinity Press International, 1991), pp. 26,52.
4. Ibid., p. 53.
5. R. A. Torrey, *The Power of Prayer* (Grand Rapids, MI: Zondervan Publishing House, 1955), p. 15.
6. Alvin Vander Griend, *The Praying Church Sourcebook* (Church Development Resources, 2850 Kalamazoo Ave., S.E., Grand Rapids, MI 49560, 1990), p. 7.
7. Richard J. Foster, *Celebration of Discipline* (San Francisco, CA: HarperSan Francisco, 1988), p. 35.
8. Brother Andrew, *And God Changed His Mind* (Grand Rapids, MI: Chosen Books, 1990), p. 15.
9. Walter Wink, *Unmasking the Powers* (Philadelphia, PA: Fortress Press, 1986), p. 91.
10. John Bisagno, *The Power of Positive Praying* (Grand Rapids, MI: Zondervan Publishing House, 1965), pp. 19,20.
11. John Calvin, *Institutes of the Christian Religion* edited by John T. McNeill (Philadelphia, PA: The Westminster Press, 1960), Book III, Chapter XX:2, pp. 864,865.
12. Judson Cornwall, *Praying the Scriptures* (Lake Mary, FL: Creation House, 1990), p. 11.

Hearing the Voice of God

O NE SATURDAY NIGHT IN 1991 WAS A RESTLESS NIGHT FOR me. I was sensing from time to time that some kind of spiritual warfare was going on. When I woke up I had a dim impression that I had dreamed about a spirit of homosexuality.

All of the above was unusual. I ordinarily sleep well and do not dream too much. Up till now, unlike many of my friends, I have not received revelations from God in dreams. And when I do have dreams I pay little or no attention to them. True to form, I did not pay much attention to this one. I have many problems in my life, but homosexuality has never even come close to being one of them.

A WORD FROM THE LORD

However, in my Sunday School class the next morning

I felt impressed to give a word to the class. This also was unusual. Over the last few years, I could count on my fingers the times I have done this. I felt it was a word from the Lord, so I spoke it publicly:

"There is someone here this morning who is being approached for a homosexual relationship, which you do not want, but which is difficult to refuse, and you need help. God will provide that help for you." I knew it was a male relationship, but I had not mentioned that part.

The next day the class treasurer, Rocky Lloyd, called me. He said that on Sunday evening he attended church and received some excellent Bible teaching. He was feeling good about the church service and went home to spend the rest of the evening studying the Bible. That evening he received phone calls from two different men, unrelated to each other, both of whom Rocky had witnessed to sometime in the past.

Action prayer is two-way prayer. We speak to God and He speaks to us, just as my earthly father and I speak to each other.

He also knew that each of them lived a homosexual life-style, and both solicited a sexual relationship with him that evening.

Although Rocky himself had no personal inclination in that direction, he called me to say that he was grateful God had warned him of it through the word He had given me, and that he praised God for arming him that same evening with the sword of the Spirit. He also said he had received direct prayer help the same morning. During the Sunday School class ministry time, without any inkling on anyone's part to whom the word from God might apply, Dave Rumph went over to Rocky and said, "God is telling me to pray for you, but I have no idea why." Dave prayed for Rocky and it was a victorious day all around.

Where did this information come from?

This obviously was an instance of direct communication from God to me and also to Dave Rumph. More importantly, through Dave and me it was a word from God to Rocky Lloyd.

In the last chapter, I mentioned that action prayer was two-way prayer. We speak to God and He speaks to us, just as my earthly father and I speak to each other when I telephone him. This should be self-evident to biblical Christians, and it is to many. But a fairly large segment of the church rather frowns on the idea that we hear from God in this day and age. People generally accept the idea that God leads us and directs us through a divine arrangement of life's circumstances, but pretending to "hear" directly from God is looked upon as not being respectable. It is particularly suspect if we in any way convey the impression that we are quoting words from God Himself, or if we are paraphrasing what we think we heard.

Was it appropriate for me to stand up in public and share what I felt was a word from God?

Was it appropriate for Dave Rumph to say, "God is telling me..."?

"JOHN MAXWELL PRAYS TODAY"

I was teaching a Fuller Seminary doctor of ministry course to around 50 pastors not long ago. To begin each day of the 2-week intensive course, I habitually call on one of the pastors as the class prayer leader and we spend around 45 minutes praying together. Earlier each morning in my personal prayer time I take out the class list and pray over my students, asking God to show me who should be the prayer leader that morning. For the first 2 or 3 days, I usually put a mark next to the names of some 10 or 15 whom I am sensing might be potential prayer leaders.

My good friend John Maxwell, pastor of Skyline Wesleyan Church in San Diego, happened to be taking the course. I did not mark his name, however, because he has such a high profile as a teacher of pastors across the country. I reasoned: (1) John does not need to be up front one more time; and (2) I do not want to be perceived as buttering up to a celebrity in our midst. I decided that others would do the praying this time.

God made a different decision. As I was praying over the marked names on the Monday morning of the second week, I clearly heard God speak in my spirit: "John Maxwell prays today." That was enough for me. I called on John Maxwell, he led, and it turned out to be the deepest and most powerful prayer time of the two weeks.

The next day John and I had dinner together. He said, "I knew you were going to call on me to pray yesterday. The night before I said to Dave Freshour, 'I'm going to pray tomorrow morning!'"

This time neither one of us shared in public what we had heard from God. But when we compared notes privately we were elated. We both identify with very conservative theological traditions, but we have both come to believe that God does speak today and that we can hear Him clearly enough to virtually quote His words. We did hear Him that time!

"AND I QUOTE"

Jack Hayford accepted this truth long before John Maxwell or I did. He says it as boldly as anyone. When he uses the term, "God spoke to me," Hayford says, "I am being even more specific than general revelation or private inner impressions. I reserve these words intentionally for the rare, special occasions when, in my spirit, I have had the Lord speak directly to me. I do not mean, 'I felt impressed' or 'I sensed somehow.'" Hayford affirms that the Lord speaks *words* to him. "Those words have been so distinct that I feel virtually able to say, 'And I quote.'"[1]

Fully recognizing my sinfulness and humanity, I feel it is proper for me to claim I am quoting the Most High God as saying to me, "John Maxwell prays today."

I am also aware that to some this will sound like sheer arrogance. "Who does Peter Wagner think he is that the Creator of the universe would stoop to speak to him?" Especially about relatively insignificant things such as resisting homosexual advances when there was probably no temptation there in the first place, or calling on a certain person to pray in a classroom.

REVELATION FROM GOD TODAY?

I fully understand this line of thinking because it was my own line for a good part of my career as an ordained minister.

In seminary, I was taught that God's general revelation was available to all humans through creation, but that His special revelation was confined to Holy Scripture. God may have spoken directly to apostles and prophets, but they wrote down what He said, and when the canon of the Old Testament and the New Testament was agreed upon, no further direct revelation was necessary. After all, Hebrews 1:1,2 says, "God, who at various times and in different ways spoke in time past to the fathers by the prophets, has in these last days spoken to us by His Son." God has said what has needed to be said. If we read and apply Scripture, we have no need for any further revelation from God.

Now I still hold a high view of biblical inerrancy, but I also realize that God has things to tell us that are not in the Bible. When I made the decision to marry Doris, for example, I had no Bible verse that told me she was the one. The same applied when I accepted the call to join the Fuller Seminary faculty. Or to invite Alice Smith to be Doris's and my I-1 intercessor.

Those who have read *Prayer Shield*, the second book in this *Prayer Warrior* series, will know that I like to make a distinction between I-1, I-2 and I-3 intercessors whom God has called to pray specifically for us and our ministry. At the moment, Doris and I have 18 I-2 and one I-1 intercessors, for a close prayer-partners team of 19. My belief is that only God chooses I-1 intercessors, so it is imperative to hear from God before establishing such a relationship.

One reason it is important for God Himself to cement this relationship is that He ordinarily will speak directly to the intercessor about the person he or she is praying for. For example, on November 15, 1990, Alice Smith wrote in her journal:

> Approximately 1:15 p.m. Houston time, there was danger for Peter Wagner. As I started to intercede, the Lord gave me a vision of a principality coming out of the south. It was as large as a man and it was hovering over Peter with an arrow in its hand pointing toward his heart. I was crying out, "Save him, Lord. Have mercy on him and save him." The Lord revealed this was a spirit of death. I asked the Holy Spirit if Peter was okay and He spoke, "His life is in the balance."
>
> Travail poured out of me! I phoned and asked Eddie [Alice's husband] to pray. As I cried for mercy, reminding the Father of His plans for Peter, speaking the Scripture and warring the forces of darkness, the Lord spoke Psalms 144 to my heart. This was a word for Peter.
>
> Then at 1:57 p.m., as quickly as this came, I saw an angel of the Lord come and take the arrow out of the principality's hand, break it over his knee, and leave westward! The spirit of death just disappeared.

What do we make of this?

Is this a woman who is emotionally disturbed and who has a hyperactive imagination? Has she been reading too much into Frank Peretti's books? Is she a fanatic on the lunatic fringe?

Not if I am a reasonable judge of character. Alice is a wonderful wife and mother. She is competent in her field of real estate. Her husband, Eddie, is a Southern Baptist pastor, and she is active in church life. She is a saintly woman and is in demand as a Bible teacher and conference speaker. She is also a nationally recognized intercessor. And she hears from God on a somewhat more regular basis than most of the rest of us.

Readers of *Prayer Shield* may recall that I told this story there including some other details. As I said in that book, I still believe that Alice's prayer saved my physical life in 1990.[2] But this time I am repeating it to underscore how crucial her ministry has been and how much some of it depends on hearing God's voice.

Writing Down What God Says

Although I do not hear directly from God too frequently, the decision to ask Alice to be our I-1 intercessor came after one of those special events. While I was having my usual morning prayer time, I found my mind being filled with thoughts that were clearly not my own. By then I was learning how to recognize God's voice, but what surprised me was the clarity with which the words themselves were coming. I took out a pencil and pad and began to write them down, realizing that it was the first time I had ever done such a thing. Here is what I wrote, with no pause whatsoever:

> You do not yet realize how important Alice Smith is going to be in doing spiritual warfare on your behalf. She will become your most powerful intercessor. You will not have a particularly close personal relationship

with her. You will not need to tell her everything she is to pray for because she is very near to me and she hears me well. I will let her know how she is to pray day by day and week by week. You do not need to reward her; her rewards will come directly from me.

I have been preparing her for this ministry, providing her special equipment, and showing her how to use it. Her name will be known and feared among the forces of evil. They will hate her and attempt to destroy her, but her sufferings will be few. Her husband will be a support and protection.

I am doing this because I have chosen you for a ministry which will require the highest level of intercession. I have been bringing new people into your life who will love you and Doris and who will fight and win spiritual battles. Many of these battles you will not even know about, but they would have destroyed you without the intercession. The intercessors will be faithful to you and you will be freed from restrictions which the enemy would bring upon you. You have suffered for me, and your suffering is largely over.

As I wrote these words, I had a sense that I was writing a form of divine revelation. It was a very important word from God at a crucial time in my life and ministry. I shared it with Alice when Doris and I invited her to be our I-1 intercessor, but so far as I can recall I have not shared it verbatim with anyone else until now.

STANDARD BRAND EVANGELICALISM

Standard brand evangelicalism has questioned the kind of behavior I have just described. "Thus saith the Lord" is all right for Isaiah or Hezekiah or the apostle Paul, but we now have something none of them had—the closed canon of Scripture. God works differently today. My theology teachers taught me to say, "We do not expect God to engage in present-day revelatory activity." Paul writes to Timothy that inspired Scripture "is profitable for doctrine, for reproof, for correction, for instruction in righteousness, that the man of God may be complete, thoroughly equipped for every good work" (2 Tim. 3:16,17).

If Scripture thoroughly equips us, so the argument goes, what more do we need? To expect to hear the voice of God today as did the prophets of old goes beyond what Scripture allows.

This line of thinking, of course, restricts any concept of prayer being two-way. Since I have learned about action prayer, I cannot talk about prayer for very long without speaking about hearing from God. But this is quite recent for me. Therefore, I am not surprised when I read an article by Billy Graham, "Power When You Pray," and see no reference at all to listening for God's voice.[3]

I do not cite this to criticize Billy Graham in any way, but simply because he is today's most visible spokesperson for our traditional evangelical stream. I also recognize that a brief article does not allow space to say everything that needs to be said about prayer, and that Graham may well believe that we do, in fact, receive present-day revelatory communication from God.

But to broaden it even more, let me refer to the Lausanne Committee for World Evangelization (LCWE), which held a massive International Prayer Assembly in Seoul, Korea, in 1984. Vonette Bright and Ben Jennings led the meeting, along with Kim Joon-Gon and Thomas Wang, which was attended by representatives of 71 countries. The program featured 94 speakers. A book was subsequently published, *Unleashing the Power of Prayer,* featuring the input of 23 of those outstanding prayer leaders.[4]

My point is this: None of these high-profile messages on prayer deals with two-way prayer or hearing the voice of God. I do not mean to imply that any or all of the speakers would deny hearing from God, but simply that it was not a high enough priority to feature in this milestone book.

RECEIVING "OVERPOWERING URGES"

When I think back to my years as a missionary, the years when I was not expecting to hear from God, I recognize that we nevertheless believed God answers prayer. We would not say to one another, "God told me so-and-so," but we would testify, for example, that God had "called me to Bolivia." Usually we would assume that the answers to prayer came in the way our subsequent circumstances were arranged by the hand of a sovereign God rather than through any direct verbal communication. But a magazine article I read recently reminded me that we were also guided by something we were allowed to call "overpowering urges."

This article was about the ministry of one of my senior missionaries in Bolivia, Bill Hammond. Back in 1950, the year of my conversion, Bill and other missionaries with the South America Mission were trying to make initial contact with the Ayoré Indians, a wild, warlike tribe, which some years previously had murdered five New Tribes Mission missionaries.

Bill Hammond, who had been praying for contact with the Ayorés, one day "felt an overpowering urge" to go to El Encanto. It would not be a natural thing to do because this would mean a grueling horseback ride of 75 miles through hostile jungle on flooded trails in the rainy season. Nevertheless, "the urge would not leave." So Bill went to look for a Bolivian coworker, Angel Bravo, whom he met coming in search of him. That morning, according to author Edith Norwood, "Angel had had the same unreasonable urge." So they made the trip, which turned out to be historic. They established the first peaceful contact with the Ayorés.[5]

There is not much question, even in the minds of standard-brand evangelicals, that Bill Hammond and Angel Bravo heard from God. God told Hammond and Bravo to go to El Encanto. Whether we call it an "overpowering urge" or a "word of knowledge," we take it as a strong enough direction from God to launch out on something as significant as a potentially life-threatening ministry journey.

This may be a matter of semantics. Maybe most evangelicals, when they think about it for a while, really do believe some kind of present-day revelatory activity is available from God.

Just don't call it "prophecy"!

THE MODERN PROPHETIC MOVEMENT

When I wrote my book *Your Spiritual Gifts Can Help Your Church Grow,* back in 1979, I was faced with a difficult decision. How would I define the gift of prophecy mentioned in Romans 12:6, 1 Corinthians 12:10 and Ephesians 4:11—the three major gift lists in the New Testament?

I had recently returned from Bolivia where we found it easier to talk about urges than words. Most of the commentaries I owned said that the gift of prophecy related to effective preaching and exposition of God's Word. But at that time I had also been doing in-depth church growth research on the Pentecostal and charismatic movements and I had begun to hear people bold enough, to use Cecil M. Robeck Jr.'s words, "to claim that he or she is speaking on behalf of God."[6]

After considerable prayer, study and consultation, I decided to go out on a limb and define it not as preaching, but as revelation. I said, "The gift of prophecy is the special ability that God gives to certain members of the Body of Christ to receive and communicate an immediate message of God to His people through a divinely-anointed utterance."[7] I have not regretted it. For one thing, I have not received the criticism I had anticipated. For another, I laid the groundwork for a biblical understanding of two-way prayer even before I had begun to practice it.

A major reason, I believe, for the absence of criticism was that just around that time the Holy Spirit began speaking to churches in general about a renewal of prophetic ministry. This had previously begun in Pentecostal and charismatic circles, but around 1980 it began spreading through evangelical and mainline traditions. At that time, a key evangelical biblical scholar, Wayne Grudem of Trinity Evangelical Divinity School, was doing his doctoral research at Cambridge University in England. Grudem's findings were later published in his influential book, *The Gift of Prophecy in the New Testament and Today.* At exactly the same time, other serious scholars such as David Hill and David Aune were researching and writing on New Testament prophecy.[8]

Wisdom for Both Camps

Wayne Grudem has words of wisdom for both camps. He comes, as I do, from the traditional evangelical camp, thus the general thrust of his book is to ask evangelicals to "give some consideration to the New Testament teachings on the gift of prophecy—and to the possibility that, in certain settings, and following scriptural safeguards, this gift may bring much personal edification and new spiritual vitality to worship."[9] As a result of Grudem's influence, together with many other similar points of light that God has used, many evangelicals are now doing what he suggests.

At the same time, Grudem appeals to Pentecostals and charismatics to be slightly less aggressive in declaring "Thus saith the Lord," unintentionally sounding as if their prophetic word is on the same level with the Bible. He points out that although they *teach* it is not on the same level, their *practice* at times makes it look that way. I believe that most thoughtful Christians from either camp would agree with Grudem when he says, "What is spoken in any prophecy today is not the word of God, but simply a human being reporting in merely human words something which God has brought to mind."[10]

Because God is speaking to the wider Body of Christ about prophecy today, our A.D. 2000 United Prayer Track, which brings together large numbers of both evangelicals and charismatics, has had to write a policy statement on the use of prophecy in interdenominational events. Although we recognize that various churches and denominations and ministries will practice prophetic ministries in different ways in their own meetings, and though we have no intention of criticizing the way others do it, we nevertheless require norms of maintaining harmony when we are all praying together. Here is the A.D. 2000 policy:

> We encourage hearing from God and using the prophetic gifts. Prudence in communicating words from God in an interdenominational meeting will avoid such phrases as "thus saith the Lord" or using the first person for God. Prophecies can be prayed back to God: "God, we hear you saying..." or expressed to the group with statements like: "I think God may be saying to us..." and expecting others to agree if it is a true word.

How has this worked? I will admit that habits are hard to break and from time to time people get emotionally caught up in a particularly fervent season of prayer and violate the rules. Most people present in such a meeting take a "so what?" attitude. We know where the other person is coming from. But in calmer moments, I have yet to meet a prayer leader who would disagree with the policy itself and who would want to violate it habitually.

An Earthquake at Fuller

I defined prophecy correctly in my 1979 book, *Your Spiritual Gifts,* but I was not ready to be involved in its application when Paul Cain landed in California on December 3, 1988. I had no way of knowing that John Wimber had invited this man, who had the reputation of a prophet, to speak to his Vineyard Ministries International leadership on the recommendation of former Dallas Seminary professor, Jack Deere. Or that this stranger from Texas had confirmed to John on the telephone that he had a message from God; an earthquake would rock Southern California the day he arrived and the epicenter would be under Fuller Seminary.

All I did know at the time was that I spent most of December 3 picking up books from my Fuller Seminary office floor and putting them back on the shelves after a 5.0 earthquake struck early that morning. The epicenter was under the Pasadena City Hall, one block from the seminary campus. Close enough!

Considering this memorable incident, my skepticism still persisted. I attended a conference at the Vineyard church in Anaheim, California, one month later in January, heard Paul Cain, and left rather unimpressed. But after Doris and I had dinner with John and Carol Wimber a couple of times that winter and spring, I became convinced that this new prophetic movement was for real.

Wayne Grudem's book, *The Gift of Prophecy*, helped me understand the prophetic movement from the evangelical side. But the book that most satisfactorily helped me understand the movement was Bill Hamon's *Prophets and Personal Prophecy.* Written from the Pentecostal perspective, Hamon's book frankly addresses both the strengths and weaknesses of the way prophecy has been taught and practiced for decades. It covers uses and abuses alike. Still, using all the proper cautions and disclaimers, Hamon affirms that God "has established the prophetic ministry as a voice of revelation and illumination which will reveal the mind of Christ to the human race."[11] I still recommend it as the best how-to book on the subject.

Cindy Jacobs' Demonstration

In early 1989 my wife, Doris, and I also met Cindy Jacobs, who, I soon learned, had logged some years of experience in prophetic ministries. We established a close friendship with Cindy and her husband, Mike, and I invited her to be the speaker at the annual retreat of our 120 Fellowship Sunday School class that fall. I asked her to teach us about prophecy.

Cindy not only taught us prophecy, but she announced to us the second day that she was going to prophesy. This was something different and slightly risky to us Congregationalists, most of whom may have heard about personal prophecy but had never been up close to it in this way. As I observed Cindy, I noticed she was following all the rules Bill Hamon had spelled out. For one thing, she insisted on having all her prophecies tape-recorded so there would be no question about what she sensed God was saying through her.

The resulting ministry was truly remarkable, and to this day many attendees date important changes in their lives to that retreat. We transcribed and published the prophecies in our *Body Life* newsletter, and in subsequent newsletters many class members shared testimonies of healing in their lives. One prophecy that Doris and I will long remember was the healing of some chronic addictions in our own nephew, Jon Mueller.

By this time I was not only convinced that personal prophecy was in effect today, but I was also comfortable in ministry settings where it was being used. One of the most notable personal experiences I have had with prophecy occurred a few months later.

SPIRITUAL DANGER TO A SEMINARY

I had gone to another state to conduct an annual ministry conference at a major theological seminary. As a professor and his wife drove me from the airport to the seminary, they told me of the remarkable spiritual renewal that had been going on in the seminary for months. I rejoiced with them, although I sensed a few yellow danger signals blinking in my mind from time to time.

As I began collecting more information, I grew somewhat alarmed. It became clear that, along with the great moving of the Holy Spirit, a high-level attack from the invisible world of darkness had been launched against the seminary, undoubtedly to nip the budding revival before it could gain much momentum. The details will remain confidential, but it was the nearest thing I had seen to a real-life enactment of Peretti's book, *This Present Darkness.*

On one of the evenings, the seminary president, whom I will call Charles, invited me to dinner with him and his wife. We had known each other for years, so we did not need to spend much time with the formalities of getting acquainted. The conversation went rapidly to the spiritual activities, both good and bad, on the campus and the picture became much clearer in my mind. After listening to Charles for about an hour, I said, "Why are you telling me this? Do you want my advice?"

"Yes," Charles said, "what would you do if you were in a situation like this?"

I said, "Charles, you and several other faculty members are caught up in a high-level spiritual conflict for which none of you has the tools to handle adequately. You're in over your heads. I don't have the tools myself; this is all quite new to me. But if I were in your situation, I know exactly what I would do: I'd call Cindy Jacobs." I explained who Cindy was and the focus of her Generals of Intercession ministry. Charles asked me if I would call Cindy on the phone to see if she would help.

When I got to my room after dinner, I called my wife, Doris, who reacted very angrily to the details I related. She agreed with me that the seminary truly was in spiritual danger, and was incensed that the evil one would employ such perverse tactics.

I then called Cindy and told her the story. She agreed that I could give Charles permission to call; he called her, and they talked for one hour. The call was a turning point for this seminary president, and a deeply moving personal experience.

"His Name Is Charles"

My third call was to Cathy Schaller, Doris's and my I-1 intercessor at the time. Here is where two-way prayer or hearing the voice of God comes into the picture.

I expected that Cathy would have been praying about my ministry at the seminar, so I gave her a brief report. Then I said that I believed God had a greater reason for taking me to that seminary. Cathy said, "You tell me what happened and then I will tell you what I have been praying about all day. It was not the seminar."

When I finished telling her what was going on at the seminary, she said she had received a word from the Lord about me during her prayer time at 9:00 that morning. It was the clearest word from God she had received about me for some time. She had been praying about it all day long, and would have called me if she had the phone number.

Among other things, the Lord had told Cathy that during the day a high-level Christian leader would approach me for some advice. *His name would be Charles!* His questions would have to do with demonization and spiritual warfare. God would give me just the right word for him. I would carry out this assignment, but it would not be an ongoing involvement for me.

Needless to say, I slept well that night, having a direct assurance from God, through the intercessor, that I had done what God wanted me to do. Hearing God clearly enough to know that my friend's name would be Charles was, to me, equivalent to predicting an earthquake.

Several other things happened, including more calls to Cindy Jacobs; needless to say the enemy was exposed and dealt with successfully. What could have been a literal disaster for the seminary was totally averted, and the revival has continued and increased. Almost three years later the seminary president says, "I am overwhelmed by the outpouring of God's blessing. Things at the seminary could not be better. Praise His name!"

In retrospect, what was the key to turning around a potentially devastating situation in a major theological seminary? I have no question that it was Cathy Schaller's intercession. This was not new or unusual for Cathy. She is a seasoned prayer leader, conference speaker and founder of Friends of the Bride-

---

Many of us are now beginning to experience two-way prayer and are hearing the voice of God. As we grow in this area, we can expect much of our rhetoric prayer to be changed to exciting action prayer.

---

groom Ministry. She practices hearing from God in her prayers and exercises a strong prophetic ministry.

HEARING FROM GOD

This seminary incident embodies the need to hear from God when we pray. Fortunately, many others throughout the Body of Christ are learning how to do this and teach it to others. A book that has become a classic on the subject is Loren Cunningham's *Is That Really You, God?* (YWAM Publishing). The subtitle is *Hearing the Voice of God.* When evangelicals ask me which book I most recommend, I tell them about Peter Lord's *Hearing God.* Writing from an evangelical point of view, Peter Lord affirms, "There is no way we can experience many of the promises of Scripture unless we know God and hear Him speaking to us."[12] He explains it well.

Many of us are now beginning to experience two-way prayer and are hearing the voice of God. As we grow in this area, we can expect much of our rhetoric prayer to be changed to exciting action prayer.

■ REFLECTION QUESTIONS ■

1. Do you know any Christians who would argue that God no longer speaks specific words to the Church in our times? What arguments do they give for their position?
2. On the other hand, do you personally know any Christians who are so sure they have heard from God that they would join Jack Hayford in saying, "And I quote"? How would they respond to those mentioned in the previous question?
3. Why do you suppose some Christians would be glad to admit that they receive "overpowering urges" from God but would not want to see this as prophetic revelation?
4. Have you personally come into contact with a prophetic ministry that could be explained only by admitting that the person must have received information supernaturally? If so, give examples.
5. Discuss the incident related to the evangelical seminary. List at least four things that the sovereign God put into place to

rescue the institution. Where did human obedience to God come in?

Notes

1. Jack W. Hayford, *Glory on Your House* (Grand Rapids, MI: Chosen Books, 1991), p. 139.
2. C. Peter Wagner, *Prayer Shield* (Ventura, CA: Regal Books, 1992), p. 154.
3. Billy Graham, "Power When You Pray," *Decision*, May 1989, pp. 1-3.
4. Vonette Bright and Ben A. Jennings, editors, *Unleashing the Power of Prayer* (Chicago, IL: Moody Press, 1989).
5. Edith Norwood, "SAM's Hall of Fame: William F. Hammond," *Windows*, April-June 1989, p. 4.
6. Cecil M. Robeck Jr., "Gift of Prophecy," *Dictionary of Pentecostal and Charismatic Movements*, edited by Stanley M. Burgess and Gary B. McGee (Grand Rapids, MI: Zondervan Publishing House, 1988), p. 738.
7. C. Peter Wagner, *Your Spiritual Gifts Can Help Your Church Grow* (Ventura, CA: Regal Books, 1979), p. 259.
8. See David Hill, *New Testament Prophecy* (Atlanta, GA: John Knox Press, 1979) and David Aune, *Prophecy in Early Christianity and the Ancient Mediterranean World* (Grand Rapids, MI: William B. Eerdmans Publishing Co., 1983).
9. Wayne Grudem, *The Gift of Prophecy in the New Testament and Today* (Westchester, IL: Crossway Books, 1988), p. 14.
10. Ibid., p. 262.
11. Bill Hamon, *Prophets and Personal Prophecy* (Christian International Ministries, P.O. Box 9000, Santa Rosa Beach, FL 32459, 1988), p. 13.
12. Peter Lord, *Hearing God* (Grand Rapids, MI: Baker Book House, 1988), p. 15.

Churches That Pray

I N CHAPTER 2, I MENTIONED THAT MY BEST GUESS WOULD be that among growing churches, the prayer ministry in 95 out of 100 would be little more or less than the prayer ministry of dozens of nongrowing churches in the same community. So far, a statistical correlation between prayer and church growth rates has not been found.

THE FIRST KEY TO CHURCH GROWTH

However, more than ever before, some of today's most outstanding, church growth pastors are affirming the importance of prayer, not simply as rhetoric but as action, for the growth of their churches. For example, when John Maxwell, pastor of Skyline Wesleyan Church in San Diego, California, which just purchased 130 acres for their new facility, lectures to pastors on

"Six Keys to Church Growth," key number one is prayer. Maxwell says, "Every time I have had a breakthrough in the growth and life of my church, it has been because of intentional prayer."

Bob Logan is known to church leaders across the country as what many consider the number-one expert in new church planting today. He is an experienced church planter himself, having started a church that grew to 1,200 and having spun off many other new churches in the process. Now he gives full time to researching, consulting, teaching and supervising church planting. When he speaks to church leaders, he outlines "The Seven Most Important Things I Have Learned About Church Planting." Number one is prayer. He says, "I agree with E. M. Bounds who said, 'Prayer is not preparation for the battle; it is the battle.'"

George Barna, one of today's most astute observers of trends in churches and society, recently researched what he calls "user-friendly churches." He identified a number of churches that stood out from the others because of the extraordinary vitality of the congregation and its positive impact on the surrounding community. Then he lists the features these churches have in common. Prayer, he found, was a foundation stone of ministry for them all. "The call to prayer," Barna says, "was the battle cry of the congregation: it rallied the troops. These people understood the power of prayer."[1]

The Wesleyan Church, a medium-size denomination, experienced a membership plateau from 1982 to 1990. However, in 1991 and 1992 attendance increased by 10 percent, and they planted more churches than in any year since the 1960s. Their Director of Evangelism and Church Growth, Marlin Mull, says:

> We attribute this breakthrough in 1989 to the beginning of a yearly emphasis during Lent called "Forty

Days of Prayer and Fasting." Churches involved in that program, or some modification of it, led the way in evangelism and church growth. Last year more than twelve-hundred of our seventeen-hundred churches participated. Prayer and church growth suggest Siamese twins. You cannot have one without eventually having the other.[2]

In my "guesstimate," I allowed for 5 churches out of the 100 that might well have a lively, dynamic prayer ministry. Such churches are the ones I am featuring in this chapter. They are examples that the other 95, at least most of them, strongly desire to follow. They are churches such as Waymon Rodgers' Christian Life Center, which I previously mentioned. Rodgers says, "The ministry of prayer is the most important of all the ministries in the church. Prayer creates the atmosphere and binds the powers of darkness so the Gospel of Jesus can go forward and the church can prosper." Sadly, he has to add: "This is the area that the majority of our churches talk about the most and practice the least."[3]

One of those pastors who has led his church in action prayer is Jack Hayford.

GLORY ON YOUR HOUSE

Jack Hayford uses the title, *Glory on Your House*, for his book on the ministry of The Church On The Way in Van Nuys, California. One of the reasons he uses this title is that the glory of God visibly appeared in the church on one occasion and opened the way for some of the most dramatic church growth in the United States.

But before the glory came, the powers of darkness had to be evicted. Not too long after Hayford began to pastor The Church On The Way, he was alone in the sanctuary when he caught a glimpse of something strange in the area around the altar. Looking into the rafters above, he briefly discerned "a small, dark, cloud-like object" and then it disappeared. He felt "a clammy presence" there. He knew then that there was an overt satanic oppression in the church and that God was calling him as the pastor to take charge and evict it. He also knew that his principal weapon would be prayer.

The particular form of prayer Hayford felt God prompting him to use was praise. Several times each week he would walk through the sanctuary, clap his hands and raise his voice aloud, declaring the honor and glory of Jesus Christ. The spirit did not leave immediately, but Jack persisted in this warfare prayer for more than a year. He can pinpoint the time of victory to a Reformation Sunday service in October. That day, through spontaneous, unplanned praise and worship on the part of the congregation, the hold of the spirit that had oppressed the church was broken.[4]

Then the way was open for the glory to come. On a Saturday afternoon when he went into the same sanctuary to adjust the thermostat, Jack Hayford suddenly noticed that the sanctuary was filled with a silvery mist. He knew it could not be natural. "No earthly dust," Hayford says, "had the glowing quality that this mist possessed as it filled the whole room, even where the sunlight was not shining." He then began to pray the two-way prayer that not only speaks, but also expects to hear from God. God's voice came clearly to him: "It is what you think it is. I have given My glory to dwell in this place."[5]

At the time, the church had been struggling and plateaued at about 100, but dramatic growth started. The next day attendance jumped to 170, and the growth has continued unabated. At this writing, The Church On The Way is approaching a weekly attendance of 10,000. Prayer is at the very heart of this explosion.

A DYNAMIC PRAYER MINISTRY FOR YOUR CHURCH

Among the churches I know that have dynamic prayer ministries, no two of them are exactly alike. But they have enough in common to discern key ingredients that should come together one way or another for maximum effectiveness. I think that the three principal human components are the pastor, the intercessors and the prayer leader. As for the program itself, training is a high priority, and then any variety of prayer ministries and activities can be put into place. The rest of this chapter will detail what I mean by this.

THE VITAL ROLE OF THE PASTOR

If I have heard John Maxwell say it once, I have heard him say it a hundred times: "Everything rises or falls on leadership." In my 25 years of professional involvement in church growth research, I have consistently found this to be true. I have also found that many Christian leaders, both clergy and laity, deeply wish this *were not* true. Many of them are in a state of denial; they somehow claim that such a concept is unbiblical.

Almost 20 years ago I wrote my first book on American church growth, *Your Church Can Grow* (Regal Books). At that time, the denial of the key role of the pastor was much stronger than it is today. Nevertheless, I went out on a limb and included a chapter, "Pastor, Don't Be Afraid of Power!" I suggested that the pastor was the first vital sign of a healthy church. Some accepted this fact more readily than others.

It is not difficult to understand why some would not want to admit that everything rises or falls on leadership. Pastors of dynamically growing churches are appropriately modest, and they do not want to take undue credit for their success. They do not want themselves to be put on a pedestal above fellow ministers who are not seeing similar growth in their churches.

Nor do they desire to underplay the role that the lay leaders and workers have in the life and growth of their church. And it goes without saying that pastors of stagnant or declining churches would prefer not to take the blame.

I love pastors. I work with them constantly. I train thousands of them each year in my Fuller Seminary classes and in conferences. I know how hard they work and how dedicated to God they are. The last thing I want to do is to lay on them a burden greater than they are able to bear. I have no desire to contribute to more pastoral frustration and burnout.

At the same time, pastors come to my classes and conferences because they know I will not sugarcoat the pill. They know that what I share with them will be the most accurate fix

The prayer ministry of the local church will rise or fall on the leadership role of the pastor.

I can get on reality at the time. Many have the love-hate relationship with me that I have with my dentist. Every time I see him he hurts me, but I like the long-term results and find it is worth the pain. My dentist is a welcome part of my life.

PASTORS AND PRAYER

I almost hate to say it, but I believe it is true: *the prayer ministry of the local church will rise or fall on the leadership role of the pastor.*

I hesitate to say it because I also teach that pastors must delegate ministry to staff members and lay leaders. Pastors who use the shepherd mode and try to do all the ministry and maintain family-type relationships with all their church members are doomed to remain under what we call the 200 barrier. To cross the 200 barrier, pastors must be willing to shift from the shepherd mode to the rancher mode and allow others to lead and manage significant ministry areas in their congregations.

Senior pastors can delegate church administration to executive pastors. They can delegate the financial matters to business managers. They can delegate music ministry, youth ministry, Christian education, visitation, weddings, pastoral care, stewardship programs, outreach and many other week-by-week church activities. In fact they *must* do this if they want the church to grow.

But the same does not apply to prayer.

The churches I have found with dynamic congregational prayer ministries have pastors who have given prayer a high enough visible priority in their lives and ministries to assume the leadership of the prayer ministry. This does not mean they themselves do all the prayer ministry. Far from it. But they do hold themselves responsible and accountable for the quantity and quality of prayer in their church. The buck stops with them. Are there ever exceptions to this? A few; but they are truly exceptions, not the rule.

MODELING PRAYER AT SKYLINE

My friend John Maxwell has modeled prayer for me. When I started researching prayer, Skyline Wesleyan in San Diego was one of the first churches I visited. Early that Sunday morning, John allowed Doris and me to observe something that the general public does not usually see. We were admitted to the empty sanctuary at 6:45 A.M., where unobtrusively we found seats in a remote pew.

Pastor Maxwell entered alone, as he does every Sunday, and began to "sanctify the sanctuary" with strategic prayer. He walked slowly up and down each aisle, laying hands on every pew. He touched the sound-control board, the altar rail, the piano, the communion table, the choir loft and the organ. He prayed over the pulpit for a longer time. At the end of one pew he stopped and knelt, then began to weep. His sobbing echoed throughout the sanctuary. God had brought to mind the special need of a family that habitually sat there in that pew and John poured out his heart in prayer for them.

At around 7:00 A.M., 3 or 4 other men began to filter in and take up the same kind of silent prayer ministry around the sanctuary. These were some of Maxwell's 100 prayer partners, a highly committed body of men who pray for their pastor daily.

This team of prayer partners is the group in Maxwell's church of more than 3,000 that has the closest personal access to the senior pastor with the exception of the church board. And no one is invited to the board who has not previously served as a prayer partner for at least a year. Not only do the prayer partners pray daily for Maxwell, but each month on their birthday date they pray all day, such as the twelfth of each month. A real estate broker, Mike Mullert, sets a special watch to beep 5 times that day and prays for John at 6:00 A.M., 10:00 A.M., 2:00 P.M., 6:00 P.M., and 10:00 P.M. If he is in a business meeting, he excuses himself when his watch beeps and prays for John in the men's room!

On one Sunday morning each month, one quarter of the prayer partners gather in Maxwell's office before the first service for a fervent prayer meeting. John shares his heart with them, then kneels as they gather around. Although Skyline would be typified as a noncharismatic Wesleyan church, the intensity and volume of this prayer time would put many Pentecostals to shame. These men know how to pray because the pastor teaches them. He schedules a Saturday morning breakfast with them three times a year and a full-day prayer retreat once a year.

Each staff member at Skyline is required to recruit, train and nurture similar groups of prayer partners. As a result, hundreds of church members engage in a regular, informed prayer ministry for their pastoral leaders. Pastors who are not willing to give prayer their highest priority need not apply for a position on John Maxwell's staff.

PASTORS PRAY FOR THEIR PEOPLE

An essential part of providing pastoral leadership for the prayer ministry of the church is to pray for the people in the congregation and to let them know you are doing so. One starting point for this might be to systematically "make mention" of each church member in prayer as Paul says he does with the Romans (see 1:9), the Ephesians (see 1:16), the Thessalonians (see 1 Thess. 1:2), and Philemon (see v. 4). But this is only a starter. More informed and consecrated prayer is the order of the day. Two of the better examples I have come across are a Presbyterian pastor and an Assemblies of God pastor.

Edward Langham Jr. is pastor of Ooltewah Presbyterian Church in Ooltewah, Tennessee. He uses the alphabetized list of his church members and prays for one church family each morning Tuesday through Friday, the days he is in the office. The week before their name will come up on the list, he sends a letter to the family, telling them what day he will be praying for them, and asking them to get any special requests to him by that time.

Ed Langham received so much positive response when he started this prayer ministry that eventually he expanded it to draw more people into the loop. He now invites the entire congregation to join him in prayer for the selected family on the appointed day. In each Sunday's church bulletin the names of the four families to be prayed for are listed according to their respective days.

As a result, the Ooltewah Presbyterian Church knows their pastor gives high priority to prayer and are reminded of it each Sunday. They feel their needs are being covered in prayer, and they themselves return the favor by praying for each other. Langham stresses the simplicity of this method, having the church secretary take care of all the details and logistics. He says, "I look forward to this ministry each week. It gives me a regular way to exercise pastoral care through prayer for every person under my responsibility."[6]

Don George pastors the dynamic Calvary Temple near Dallas, Texas, one of the nation's largest Assemblies of God churches. He uses a system of praying for his church's people that he first got from the late L. D. "Bill" Thomas of First United Methodist Church in Tulsa, Oklahoma. Don writes a letter to his people, informing them that he is leaving on a certain date for a four-day prayer retreat all by himself. Don's only agenda is to intercede for the people at Calvary Temple. He sends them a return envelope marked "Confidential" and a sheet of paper headed: Pastor George, please pray for this need.

Don tells them, "The letter you write will not be opened until I am alone with God. I will open your letter personally, and pray over your request personally. After I have prayed, your letter will be destroyed. Only three persons will know what you have written: yourself, myself, and God." According to Don George, prayer retreats such as this bring in many victory reports, and he attributes much of the health and vitality of the congregation to answers to these prayers.

Although his church is so large that George could not possibly pray with his people one-on-one, they feel personally prayed for by their senior pastor. And they also know for sure that their pastor gives high priority to prayer.

THE NEGLECTED POWER OF INTERCESSORS

If the intercessors God has placed in each congregation would be recognized, coordinated, trained and released for ministry, churches across America and the world could be completely turned around. Unfortunately, many Christians, including pastors, do not realize that the intercessors are there, nor are they equipped to recognize them. The second book in this *Prayer Warrior* series, *Prayer Shield*, was written to help connect pastors and other Christian leaders with intercessors and to elicit the support of the rest of the Body of Christ.

I will not attempt to repeat what is written in *Prayer Shield*, but I will reiterate that, though I find no Scripture that explicitly teaches it, I am personally convinced God has given the spiritual gift of intercession to certain members of the Body of Christ. All Christian people are expected to pray and to intercede for others, just as all Christians are expected to be active witnesses for Jesus Christ. But God has selected some to have a special prayer ministry, using the gift of intercession, just as He has selected some to have the gift of evangelism.

It is these gifted people to whom I am referring in this section. If a church-wide prayer ministry is to take root and grow, it will do so much more readily if the gifted intercessors are actively praying it into being.

A fairly detailed profile of intercessors is found in *Prayer Shield*. One of the first things to look for is people who pray from 2 to 5 hours a day and enjoy it. That seems almost impossible to most Christians, but not to intercessors. My untested calculation is that in an average life-giving church of 100 members, 5 or 6 will have the gift of intercession. It is possible that some will have the gift but have not yet recognized it. Others will affirm it immediately.

Most intercessors fit roughly into four ministry emphases: general intercessors, crisis intercessors, personal intercessors and warfare intercessors. Some will minister from time to time in up to all four of the areas. Others will minister mostly in one area. Pastors who desire to spark action prayer ministries in their church will identify the intercessors, meet with them, share with them, listen to them and challenge them to invade the invisible world on behalf of the prayer atmosphere in the church as a whole. Powerful results can be expected, especially when they begin hearing from God together.

"I WANT TO WATCH YOU DIE"

Ted Haggard, pastor of the 4,000-member New Life Church of Colorado Springs, Colorado, is one who has moved his church into action prayer, and one who has developed a deep appreciation of the ministry of intercession.

A frightening thing happened to Ted Haggard on a Tuesday early in 1992. A man from his church whom he had known for years sat down with Ted in the pastor's study. Soon, much to Ted's alarm, a cold attitude of hatred came out of the man. He declared he would enjoy killing Haggard. He knew that killing the pastor would ruin his family and his standing in the community, but he said that the joy of seeing Ted die would be worth it.

Ted knew enough about the man to know that he was an avid hunter who was used to killing and that he had a veritable arsenal of weapons in his home. With his cold, ruthless demeanor he could have easily taken out a weapon and committed murder. His intensity mounted as he called Ted names and cursed Ted's children. Then, unexplainably, he relaxed a bit, said the Holy Spirit would not let him go any further, and left. Before he left, he also affirmed that he had not yet decided whether or not he would obey the Holy Spirit.

Soon afterward Ted learned the rest of the story. A group of intercessors from another church led by Bill Anderson, who also happens to be one of Doris's and my personal prayer partners, was praying the previous Tuesday. The group meets every Monday through Friday and prays from 12:00 noon to 1:00 P.M. On that Tuesday, they received a particular burden to pray for Ted Haggard. Ted asked Bill to put in writing what had happened, and this is what he said:

> When I was in intercession I had a picture of this man who had easy access to you from your congregation. He had a spirit of violence and murder on him. We started interceding and travailing and binding the plans that this man had for your harm. I quoted the Scripture: "Jesus came to paralyze the works of the devil," and we felt like, when we were released from interceding, we had really won. We felt we had paralyzed the works of the devil and bound them up.[7]

The upshot is that the man with the murderous spirit has now repented. He sold his guns, and is joyfully attending the church services. Intercession made the difference!

Nothing could be more important for a pastor who wants to see increased power of God in the ministry than to have a group of personal prayer partners committed to pray regularly. If the group includes gifted intercessors called to personal intercession, so much the better. How to organize and maintain such a group is the principal theme of *Prayer Shield*, so I will not repeat it here.

INSTALLING A PRAYER LEADER

Although I believe it is the ultimate responsibility of the senior pastor of a church to assume the leadership of the prayer ministry, the management of the ministry should ordinarily be delegated to a prayer leader. The larger the church, the more necessary this is.

Many people do not realize that all gifted intercessors are not potential prayer leaders. Interestingly enough, not all prayer leaders have the spiritual gift of intercession. I myself am an example of this.

I coordinate what is currently the largest network of prayer networks in the world under the A.D. 2000 United Prayer Track, I write books on prayer, I teach about prayer, I am totally committed to prayer, I understand intercessors and love them and need them for my ministry, but I am not one of them. My personal prayer life might be above average, but if so, it is only slightly above average. The major reason I see the fruit I do in my ministry is because God has given me several who do have the spiritual gift of intercession as members of Doris's and my close circle of prayer partners.

"Allow yourself and your church to take prayer as seriously as you take education, worship, outreach, and fellowship."

The ideal combination is to name a prayer leader who also has the gift of intercession. This is what I have done for the intercession teams working directly with my prayer track. Bobbye Byerly of Women's Aglow and Bill Anderson, whom I just mentioned, are the leaders of one team of 60 intercessors for the Spiritual Warfare Network. Ben Jennings of Campus Crusade and Bobbye Byerly lead another team of 120 for the whole track. They are responsible for the personnel on their teams, the agendas, the schedules, the style of prayer, the discipline and the troubleshooting necessary. But they all report to me.

It is very important for a local church to have a designated prayer leader. Sometimes this person is called a prayer coordinator or a prayer director. A growing number of churches are opening full-time staff positions for a pastor of prayer or minister of prayer. I agree with Alvin Vander Griend who says, "Allow yourself and your church to take prayer as seriously as you take education, worship, outreach, and fellowship. The resulting outpouring of prayer will enrich all of your ministries with God's vision and power."[8]

Pastors who create staff positions or top-level lay leadership positions for prayer leaders send a strong message throughout the congregation that prayer is a high priority. Too often prayer is looked upon as a by-product of doing church. It is something that is supposed to happen automatically. It is free. It requires no special effort nor line item in the budget. Obviously, that kind of an attitude is a sure formula for a church where most talk about prayer is rhetoric and where the results of prayer are virtually nil.

In these days of the great prayer movement sweeping across our nation and around the world, the emergence of exciting possibilities for new and vital prayer ministries in the church is limitless. Churches that hope to have an ear to hear what the Spirit is saying must have a prayer leader who is both called and committed to hearing these things and who is motivating others to full participation.

This is not a job for the church wimp. Alvin Vander Griend lists the following qualifications for a local church prayer leader:

- A strong personal prayer life;
- Spiritual maturity;
- Gifts to organize, encourage and give leadership in prayer;
- A good reputation in the congregation and the confidence of church leaders;

- Enough time to attend key prayer events in the church and the community.[9]

TEACHING THE CHURCH TO PRAY

A few churches that take prayer seriously and are large enough to have access to resources have installed semiformal training programs to teach their people to pray. These "schools of prayer" are presently too few and far between, but as the prayer movement spreads they will become more numerous.

One of the pioneers of developing what they call, boldly enough, "College of Prayer" is the Community Church of Joy in Phoenix, Arizona. My friend Walt Kallestad is among the most innovative Evangelical Lutheran Church of America pastors today, and as such leads a congregation of some 7,000 at this writing. In 1989, the church was adding 50 new members a month, but one year later in 1990 the rate had doubled to 100 a month. "What has made the difference?" asks Kallestad. "The answer is intentional, committed prayer and intercession."[10]

The change at Community Church came during a course in Walt's Fuller Seminary doctoral program when a class discussion was held on personal prayer partners for pastors. He and his church were agonizing before God for a new vision at that time. Walt says, "My stomach was continually raw from the constant churning."

Walt went to his hotel room that afternoon and decided to fast and pray. His usual brief prayer time extended to several hours. He felt he was in touch with the heart of God, and he emerged from the prayer time with a clear vision for the church that seemed deceptively simple. "The answer," Walt says, "was to put prayer in the highest possible priority in my own life as well as the life of Community Church of Joy."[11]

Among other things, Walt recruited a team of 30 personal

prayer partners and set a goal for 100. Then he opened a staff position for a man in his church who had a proven record as an intercessor and prayer leader, Bjorn Pedersen, to become a full-time pastor of prayer.

THIRTY-EIGHT COURSES ON PRAYER

Bjorn Pedersen has developed one of the most advanced local church schools of prayer I have seen. He says, "The purposes of the College of Prayer are to increase believers' awareness of the need to pray, provide practical tools for how to pray, and encourage people *to pray*."[12]

The school's catalog lists 38 courses running from 1 session to 13 sessions each, taught in fall, winter and spring quarters. The cost is $1.00 a class hour and a minimum of $5.00 a course. Pedersen has developed study programs that qualify students for the Bachelor's Certificate of Prayer, the Master's Certificate of Prayer and the Doctor's Certificate of Prayer. I am sure the courses are not accredited by the Association of Theological Schools, but I am equally sure they are accredited by God.

Bjorn travels around the country training prayer leaders not only in the organization of prayer schools for their churches, but in many other exciting local church prayer ministries.

Your church may not have the resources to start a full-fledged prayer school; nevertheless, part of the prayer leader's job description must be to develop regular training programs of some kind to teach people to pray. Children need to learn to pray, and when they do learn, many pray powerfully. Families need to learn to pray together, and husbands and wives with each other. Church members need to learn to pray with prayer partners, in prayer triplets, in home prayer cells or in their private devotions. Members of church boards and committees need to learn how to spend more of their meeting time in prayer and less time in discussions about what so often turns out to be trivial decisions.

All of this can be done if the senior pastor prioritizes prayer, installs a competent prayer leader, and maintains personal leadership to see that adequate resources and support of every kind are provided to make the prayer ministry one of the most high-profile ministries in the church.

BUILDING A PRAYER MINISTRY

The components of a dynamic, church prayer ministry will vary from church to church, but the menu for selecting them is growing rapidly. Later on in the book I will deal separately with corporate prayer and prayer in the community. But here I will limit myself to describing six of the more common other forms of prayer ministry currently enjoying a good deal of popularity in local churches that give prayer a high priority.

1. Twenty-four-hour prayer ministries. Pastor Ed Young of Second Baptist Church, Houston, Texas, always knew that a local church should be a house of prayer. He looks back at the year 1982 when Second Baptist established a formal prayer ministry, and some of the nation's most explosive church growth began at that time. Now, depending on how one measures it, Second Baptist can be considered the largest Southern Baptist congregation in the nation. Ed Young firmly believes that God has honored the church's strong commitment to prayer.

Among many other prayer activities, Second Baptist has one of the most outstanding 24-hour prayer ministries. Jill Griffith is the church's full-time Prayer Ministry Director. She is both an intercessor and a prayer leader and directs lay leaders, intercessors and volunteer church members who are involved in the many facets of the prayer ministry. A full-time secretary and many volunteers keep track of myriad details associated with praying for the needs of the large congregation and its community.

The prayer ministry facilities include a prayer room that has two work stations separate from each other. One is for the intercessor who receives prayer requests over the telephone, and the other is for a silent intercessor who prays for existing requests as well as for the one ministering on the telephone. This prayer room is staffed 24-hours a day. Each intercessor is asked to serve one hour a week to fill the 168 hours in a week. Having two intercessors in the prayer room for each hour during the week in addition to substitutes who are on call when needed, more than 390 church members are involved in this part of the ministry, which is referred to as the "First Watch."

More recently a "Second Watch" has been formed; here intercessors commit to pray weekly during a designated hour and day from wherever they are, to provide a 24-hour "prayer blanket" for the whole Second Baptist family. Separate 24-hour watches are organized for the north, south, east and west sections of greater Houston. This means that a minimum of 672 (168 hours a week times 4) volunteers participate weekly in this exciting prayer activity.

2. Prayer rooms. Essential to a 24-hour prayer watch is a physical prayer room. Many churches are remodeling old facilities such as unused chapels or designing new facilities to provide floor space necessary for a designated prayer center for the church.

Terry Teykl has seen Aldersgate United Methodist Church of College Station, Texas, grow from 6 to more than 1,200 in attendance. He is one of the foremost researchers and teachers on prayer in our day. He has recently written an excellent book, *Making Room to Pray*. In it he explains how to develop a prayer center in your church to help win your city for God. He suggests that this be separate from the prayer room used to house a 24-hour telephone ministry.

The prayer center Teykl envisions is designed to:

- Keep vital information available to help people pray in an informed manner;
- Provide inspirational places where people can come individually or as a group to pray;
- Visually remind people of the importance of intercession in the local church for targeted sites in the community; and
- Help develop a praying discipline in the local church to fuel other prayer ministries in the church.[13]

At this writing, 50 churches Terry Teykl has contacted now have prayer rooms.

3. Prayer chains. As Alvin Vander Griend says, "A prayer chain is the alarm system for the needs of the congregation. It makes possible a concentrated prayer effort on any specific concern or issue, including emergency situations."[14]

Vander Griend specifically says, "including emergency situations," because it is a mistake to project the image that a church prayer chain is *only* for emergencies. Experience shows that when this happens there is a tendency to use the prayer chain less and less and it can die a slow death.

The usual way to organize a prayer chain is to create a list of prayer chain members including telephone numbers. It starts with the leader or captain of the prayer chain who calls the next person on the list. If there is no answer, the next one in line is called until the entire prayer chain is informed of the need. Later, those who received no answer call those whom they skipped again, but in the meantime the chain has not been broken

No one should be encouraged to join a prayer chain who is not: (1) committed to pray immediately after the request is received; (2) committed to making telephone calls until another member of the chain is reached; or (3) committed to repeating the request exactly, word for word. Anything else will be a weak link.

Small churches may have only one prayer chain. Larger churches can have several. Whether the church is large or small, the church prayer leader needs to take responsibility for recruitment, maintenance and quality control of the prayer chain. This, of course, can be delegated to another person, but it must be closely monitored or it will wither. One principle for keeping a prayer chain going is to keep using it. Like a human muscle, the more it is used the stronger it gets. Church prayer chains that do not activate at least once a week are in danger.

One other principle for maintaining the vitality of prayer chains is to design and implement an efficient way to share answers to prayer with prayer chain members. Without answers to prayer, the ministry can become tedious.

4. Prayer retreats. When prayer becomes an important part of the life of a congregation, pray-ers and intercessors will want to enjoy extended periods of time to pray together in prayer retreats.

For one thing, a prayer retreat should be fundamentally for prayer, and not a catchy name for another conference. Teaching should be on aspects of prayer. A large proportion of time should be spent on actually praying, including praise and worship in song. Some praying should be corporate, some in groups and some individual. Sharing is important, but the time given to sharing must not overshadow the time for bringing the requests before God.

The church prayer leader should be skilled at leading prayer retreats. If this skill needs to be developed, funds should be made available for training seminars or apprenticeship visits to seasoned retreat leaders. Once the church prayer leader develops these skills, they should be taught to others in the church.

Bjorn Pedersen of the Community Church of Joy holds

prayer retreats for prayer leadership, church leadership, families and some for all in the congregation who are interested. Various groups in the church can also schedule their own prayer retreats from time to time.

5. Prayer weeks. Many churches schedule annual or twice-a-year events to feature certain ministries. Our church, for example, has a missions week, a week to emphasize lay ministry and another week to emphasize local outreach. Why not do the same for prayer?

Given the multiple ideas that are being shared among prayer leaders in our country these days, this could truly be an exciting week. On the first Sunday, invite an outstanding prayer leader to challenge the congregation—undoubtedly your area has one. Design the week's program by planning powerful prayer events. On the final Sunday, the pastor wraps it up by presenting a message on prayer and using special prayer in the worship service.

This again sends a message throughout the entire congregation that prayer is a high priority in your church. It should get a five-star rating in the church program.

6. Specialized prayer teams. Most churches have specialized ministries. Prayer teams should be organized with pray-ers who feel a particular burden for certain ministries, and they should be activated and maintained. Many churches are doing this, and some of the most frequent specialized prayer teams include:

- **Evangelism.** They pray for whatever evangelistic activities the church might have, for the people involved in frontline evangelism, and for an increased burden in the church for evangelism. When the Evangelism Explosion program experimented with intentionally recruiting evangelism prayer teams to pray for those who went out to minister, the number of professions of faith doubled!

- **World missions.** Not everyone is turned on by missions, but those who are world Christians are. Each church needs a strong missions prayer team. Many churches have organized a Frontier Fellowship and are fed prayer requests and answers to prayer by the United States Center for World Mission in Pasadena, California.
- **Healing.** An increasing number of churches, both charismatic and noncharismatic, are now organizing teams of people skilled in praying for physical and emotional healing. My book *How to Have a Healing Ministry in Any Church* (Regal Books) has helped many churches move into this area of compassion and fruitfulness.
- **Deliverance.** A growing awareness is taking place in the entire Body of Christ of the pernicious activity of Satan and the demon forces he controls. Many are realizing that this is a problem here in America as well as in the Third World. All too few churches in any given city have those who are trained to cast out demons and deliver people according to biblical patterns. Charles Kraft's book *Defeating Dark Angels* (Servant Publications) is highly recommended as a guide. May teams specializing in deliverance prayer multiply!
- **Worship service.** Many churches are recruiting teams who will specialize in praying through the various worship services of the church. Sometimes this is done in separate rooms using closed circuit TV or a speaker system. Sometimes the pray-ers kneel behind the speaker's platform or nearby. Spurgeon had large groups of intercessors praying in a basement room *under* his pulpit in each service and said it was his divine "furnace room."

SUMMARY

Obviously, this chapter only scratches the surface on the possibilities for vital prayer ministries in the local church. Many of the titles you will find in the endnotes will give further instruction and suggestions. Some of you will notice that I did not mention the corporate prayer life of the church in this chapter, and that is because I think it is important enough to merit a chapter of its own. (See chapter 5.)

For Immediate Action.
If you feel God is moving you toward initiating a strong prayer ministry in your church, I recommend that you start by ordering these two highly practical items:
1. *The Praying Church Sourcebook* compiled by Alvin J. Vander Griend. Church Development Resources, 2850 Kalamazoo Ave., S.E., Grand Rapids, MI 49560.
2. *Church Prayer Ministry Manual* compiled by T. W. Hunt, Southern Baptist Convention Press, 127 Ninth Avenue, North, Nashville, TN 37234.

■■ REFLECTION QUESTIONS ■■

1. Several churches that have outstanding prayer ministries are mentioned in this chapter. Do you know of any others that might be included? What aspects of prayer seem to set them apart?
2. Is it going too far to say that the major factor determining the prayer life of a congregation is the modeling of its pastor? Could others in the church develop a dynamic prayer ministry if the pastor was reluctant or simply indifferent?
3. Peter Wagner speaks of "gifted intercessors." What would

be the characteristics of such people? Can you name someone you know who might fit this description?

4 Is it legitimate to pay a person to pray or to lead a church
prayer ministry? Aren't all Christians supposed to pray and
not expect material rewards for praying?

5. Review the six forms of prayer ministry that are becoming
popular in many churches. What are some other ways that
prayer is implemented in churches today? Are any of these
active in your church? Should they be?

Notes

1. George Barna, *User Friendly Churches* (Ventura, CA: Regal Books, 1991), p. 116.
2. Marlin Mull, personal letter to C. Peter Wagner, January 25, 1993.
3. Waymon Rodgers, "The Seed of Prayer in Church Growth," *Church Growth*, September 1987, p. 19.
4. Jack Hayford, *Glory on Your House* (Grand Rapids, MI: Chosen Books, 1991), pp. 63-67.
5. Ibid., pp. 13-16.
6. Personal letter to Peter Wagner from Edward Langham Jr., March 8, 1989.
7. Personal letter from Ted Haggard to Peter Wagner, March 18, 1992.
8. Alvin Vander Griend, *The Praying Church Sourcebook* (Grand Rapids, MI: Church Development Resources, 1990), p. 9.
9. Ibid., pp. 5,6.
10. Walt Kallestad, *The Intercessor*, Fall 1990, p. 1.
11. Ibid.
12. *Community Church of Joy College of Prayer Catalog*, 1990-1991, p. 3.
13. Terry Teykl, *Making Room to Pray* (Renewal Ministries, Inc., 6501 East Highway 6 Bypass, College Station, TX 77845, 1991), back cover.
14. Vander Griend, *The Praying Church*, p. 52.

Some Do's and Don'ts of Corporate Prayer

"CORPORATE PRAYER," THE WAY I AM USING THE TERM, means simply that the members of a local church meet together for the purpose of praying. It is parallel to corporate *worship,* which usually takes place every Sunday morning. I do not mean that prayer and worship should not take place as a part of many other church activities as well. They should and do. But one of the most significant aspects of the total prayer ministry of the church as a whole can be calling the congregation or a significant part of the congregation together for corporate prayer.

THE WEDNESDAY NIGHT PRAYER MEETING

Generations ago, Wednesday night became the most commonly designated time of the week for corporate prayer. Almost every church of almost every denomination was expected to conduct a weeknight prayer meeting. This tradition continues in many churches today. Despite the fact that hardly anyone goes to their prayer meeting, many churches would think they were backslidden if they did not hold it every week.

At the turn of the century, R. A. Torrey said, "The prayer meeting ought to be the most important meeting in the church. It is the most important meeting if rightly conducted."[1]

It is hard to disagree with Torrey. But church leaders today are frustrated. Many churches today have discontinued weekly prayer meetings. Many that still have them admit the meetings have become routine, dull and lifeless, generating little action prayer either for the church or for the community.

One of the reasons for the frustration may be that pastors do not "rightly conduct" their prayer meetings, as Torrey would say. It comes as a surprise for some lay leaders in the church to learn that their pastors were never taught in seminary how to lead corporate prayer.

For years, the only seminary I knew of that offered even one course in prayer was Asbury Theological Seminary in Kentucky. Fortunately, given the influence of the great prayer movement, this is now changing. But most pastors in the ministry today never took such a course nor do they even have a book in their library on the church's corporate prayer meeting. Other books may be around, but the research I have done on prayer has turned up only one such work so far. It is a wonderful book by Sue Curran, *The Praying Church: Principles and Power of Corporate Prayer.*[2] Unfortunately, it has not enjoyed the wide circulation that it should have.

Is there hope for corporate prayer? Yes, indeed. Alvin Vander Griend reports that some churches in America have "prayer meetings that are bursting at the seams with people and filled with fervent prayer—meetings where people come expecting to be changed and to encounter God. The church parking lots are crowded, rooms filled to overflowing, people profess their faith, some are converted or healed, and specific answers to prayer come every week."[3]

I fully recognize that God may not lead each and every church to make corporate prayer a central part of their philosophy of ministry, but many churches today are heading in that direction. The Bible certainly encourages us to do it.

CORPORATE PRAYER IN SCRIPTURE

If the Church was born on the day of Pentecost, it was born out of corporate prayer. Before Jesus left His disciples on earth, He told them to gather in Jerusalem, "Until you are endued with power from on high" (Luke 24:49). They followed His instructions and met together in the Upper Room. What were they doing there? We are told that they "all continued with one accord in prayer and supplication" (Acts 1:14).

Their prayers were dramatically answered by the coming of the Holy Spirit on the day of Pentecost. According to the Scripture, being in prayer "in one accord" played some role in the outpouring of spiritual power that day.

The Church was established and normal church life began. The first biblical description of what New Testament Christians do in church is given in the second chapter of Acts. "And they continued steadfastly in the apostles' doctrine and fellowship, in the breaking of bread, and *in prayers*" (Acts 2:42, emphasis mine). Corporate prayer was not peripheral back then as it often is now. It was central.

Soon afterward when Peter was thrown into prison awaiting execution, a sustained, corporate prayer meeting was held. "Peter was therefore kept in prison, but constant prayer was offered to God for him by the church" (Acts 12:5). We are later told (see Acts 12:12) that the prayer meeting was convened in the house of Mary, the mother of Mark, recalling that because there were no church buildings in those days, all meetings of the congregations were held in homes. The result, of course, was that Peter was miraculously freed from prison by an angel.

Jesus declared that the Temple of God should be a "house of prayer" (see Matt. 21:13). I believe that is still God's wish for churches. Each church should be a center of prayer not only for the congregation but also for the community. Some truly are, and as we move through the decade of the 1990s, more and

---

There is evidence that the quantity of prayers is important. The more pray-ers, the more agreement. The more who pray, the more the potential power.

---

more churches are joining their ranks. God is bringing a new awareness of prayer throughout the Body of Christ, and this is one reason many have begun to say that revival might be right around the corner.

THE POWER OF AGREEMENT

The chief quality that corporate prayer has over other kinds of prayer is agreement. Jesus said, "If two of you agree on earth concerning anything they ask, it will be done for them by My Father in heaven" (Matt. 18:19). Agreement in prayer among 2 or 200 is more effective than the solitary prayers of an individual Christian, although such prayers must not be neglected or underestimated. No prayer is wasted. Corporate prayer, however, builds agreement more than any other kind of local church prayer.

There is evidence that the quantity of pray-ers is important. The more pray-ers, the more agreement. Sue Curran says, "When we move from praying alone to praying corporately, we move into a realm in which results are calculated exponentially. We move from the realm of addition to that of multiplication: for every person added, the prayer power is multiplied."[4]

Sue cites two Old Testament Scriptures to illustrate the principle. "Five of you shall chase a hundred, and a hundred of you shall put ten thousand to flight" (Lev. 26:8). And, "How could one chase a thousand, and two put ten thousand to flight?" (Deut. 32:30). These obviously should not be used as mathematical formulas to calculate the power of church prayer meetings, but nevertheless the principle is there. The more who pray, the more the potential power.

Many church leaders use Hebrews 10:25, "not forsaking the assembling of ourselves together, as is the manner of some," to encourage attendance at the weekly worship service. This is certainly a legitimate application, but the context also indicates that it should be applied to gathering for prayer. The previous verses teach the priesthood of all believers: through the blood of Jesus not just some high priest, but *all of us* have access directly to God. We must not forsake the assembling of ourselves together as priests who communicate directly with God in prayer.

ARENAS FOR CORPORATE PRAYER

There are two basic arenas for corporate prayer. The largest is on a community level where a number of churches in the community gather in concerts of prayer. This is extremely important, more important than many of us currently think. I will deal with community corporate prayer in more detail in the next chapter.

The other arena is the most common one—the local church. The balance of this chapter will deal with some of the how-to's of local church corporate prayer. To help separate it from the many other possible prayer activities of the church, I am focusing, as I have said, on *meetings scheduled by and for the church as a whole primarily for prayer.* Although much prayer is used in many Sunday worship services, I am excluding these from the corporate prayer meetings.

ACTIVITY	Corporate prayer ranks		
	Higher	Equal	Lower
Music/Worship			
Pastoral care			
Evangelism			
Christian education			
Youth programs			
Preaching			
Koinonia/fellowship			
World missions			
Community outreach			
Small groups			

How important is corporate prayer in our church life? How can we measure and report this? I believe we can take two practical measurements, one subjective and one objective.

Subjective measurement. Q: How does corporate prayer rank in our value system compared to 10 other common church activities?

Because this measurement is admittedly subjective, it might or might not be revealing. Particularly those church leaders who proclaim that the midweek prayer meeting is the most important meeting of the week, regardless of the overt interest in and quality of that meeting, would invariably tend to rank the value of corporate prayer on the high end of the scale. That is why we should also take a more objective measurement.

Objective measurement. Q: How does corporate prayer rank with the church activities mentioned above in terms of:

- Budget allocation?
- Staff time based on job descriptions?
- Time set aside on the weekly church calendar?
- Measurable church goals? I cannot count the number of churches I have seen that conscientiously set annual measurable goals for the life and growth of their church, but totally neglect setting any goals for corporate prayer. Considering the spread of the great prayer movement, promising changes have already begun to take place.
- Sermon time? Of the approximately 45 annual sermons the senior pastor preaches in the central weekly worship service, how many are explicitly and primarily on prayer?

These questions lend themselves to numerical answers. By using them, churches can accurately evaluate themselves, and, if they become courageous enough, can also compare themselves to similar churches in their denominations or communities.

How Important Are Numbers?

For many varieties of prayer, large numbers are not important. Relatively few people can and do provide powerful prayer support. For example, Doris and I have only 19 members of the inner circles of our prayer partners team, and we are not particularly looking for more. The prayer support we receive from them is incredible and it seems to be the number God is indicating for us at the moment.

The situation changes, however, when we deal specifically with *corporate* prayer. If a local church feels that corporate prayer should be a central part of their philosophy of ministry, the number of church members who participate becomes very important. In some cases it might turn out to be one of the best barometers of the spiritual quality of the church as a whole.

A Measuring Scale

Most of us are not in the habit of measuring prayer; thus we have not come to general agreement as church leaders on how to quantify the corporate prayer life of our churches. My suggestion is very simple: *Calculate the percentage of those who attend the weekly worship service and who also return to the church at least one other time during the week for corporate prayer.*

If we calculate this over a period of time, we can easily gauge how our own congregation is doing. But how might this compare with other churches, especially those that are strongly stressing corporate prayer? To answer this question, I researched several churches that were known to me as having especially strong prayer ministries at the time. I say "at the time," because I have also learned that prayer takes a roller-coaster pattern in many churches. I believe the devil concentrates attacks more on the prayer ministry of churches than any other ministry, a fact that in itself ought to tell us how important prayer is.

Here is some of what I found in my research:

- The church in the United States that had the highest percentage of worship attenders return for corporate prayer was the Alamo City Baptist Church in San

Antonio, Texas. Frances Smyth, the church prayer ministry coordinator, says, "Pastor David Walker has led us for nearly four years in an exciting and rewarding prayer adventure."[5] When I took the measurement at Alamo City, 66 percent of the 2,000 worship attenders were involved in weekly corporate prayer. By 1993, they had mobilized a Prayer Army of 560 Watchmen/Warriors.

- The Metro Vineyard church of Kansas City is pastored by Mike Bickle, one of America's foremost teachers and practitioners of intercession. Corporate prayer is so important in the Metro Vineyard that the job description of each staff member requires them to attend at least one corporate prayer meeting *a day*. My spot-check there indicated that 43 percent of the 3,500 attenders returned for corporate prayer.
- When Larry Lea had his high-profile, early-morning, corporate prayer meetings going at Church on the Rock in Rockwall, Texas, some 24 percent of the 5,000 attenders were participating.
- John Wimber's church, Vineyard Christian Fellowship of Anaheim, California, strongly stresses corporate prayer. When I tested it, 13 percent were involved.
- In our area of Southern California, the church that has the reputation for the most lively Wednesday-night prayer meeting is Jack Hayford's The Church On The Way. On an average, 29 percent of their Sunday worshipers attend these meetings.

THE BASIC INGREDIENTS FOR CORPORATE PRAYER

For churches that desire to see corporate prayer come alive and become a dynamic ministry center in their church, I see five basic ingredients.

1. The pastor. The senior pastor must take direct charge of the corporate prayer ministry of the church. The day-to-day implementation of various aspects of the prayer ministry can be delegated to the church prayer leader and others, but if the pastor is not perceived by the congregation as the supreme leader of corporate prayer, it will not fly as it should. I agree with Sue Curran who says, "My own conviction formed from personal experience and considerable study of revival history is

---

Pastors should build excitement about prayer in their churches by regularly sharing answers to prayer from the pulpit.

---

that the pastor's example must be the initiating force in the prayer ministry of the church."[6]

How should this be done? The pastor must make constant use of the pulpit to highlight the priority of prayer and the corporate prayer program. Teaching on prayer should flow regularly from the pastor as both major and minor themes. All communication systems of the church should be activated to remind people of corporate prayer. Most importantly, the pastor must set an example by regularly participating in the church corporate prayer activities along with the spouse and family. An outstanding example of this is the Korean pastors I previously described who personally attend every predawn prayer meeting because "that is where the power is!"

Pastors should build excitement about prayer in their churches by regularly sharing answers to prayer from the pulpit. Many pastors will go for a year without once sharing anything dramatic that happened in their own lives because of prayer, at the same time telling their people they should pray and expect dramatic answers. Also, time should regularly be made in the weekly worship service for testimonies of church members who have seen recent prayers answered. This has a powerful effect, particularly by having the pastor on the same platform nodding approval.

2. *The church staff.* This may seem somewhat radical, but if corporate prayer is as important as we say it is, every church staff member should be required to participate in at least one corporate prayer event a week. Also program staff (as contrasted to support staff) should be encouraged to involve their spouses and children in corporate prayer.

Some staff who are gifted for the ministry should be assigned to lead corporate prayer. At the same time, some other staff should not. I have seen examples where leading corporate prayer was assigned to staff across the board, having discouraging results because the person's gifts of the Holy Spirit were not openly recognized.

Many senior pastors of praying churches lead most of the corporate prayer, but not all. I was impressed by a pastor of a large church in Christchurch, New Zealand, who recognized that the church prayer leader, a woman, was much more gifted to lead corporate prayer than he was. He attended every meeting, but she took charge. She would meet with a small group of intercessors that afternoon and pray until God revealed to them His agenda for the evening prayer meeting. The result was one of the best-attended and most exciting weeknight prayer meetings I have attended.

3. *Location.* It is advisable to use the same physical location for the corporate prayer activities the church uses for regular worship. I am obviously not referring to the same room because the sanctuary will usually be too large. But people should get used to praying together where they go to worship.

4. Time. A consensus I have found is that one hour is the ideal time period for a corporate prayer meeting, at least in most parts of the United States. In our culture, people will respond better if the meetings start and end promptly. The time of day will vary, depending on when people are available. Many churches in the United States are finding early morning prayer to be effective, although I do not think it can, as yet, be called a trend. The number of times corporate prayer meetings are held each week depends on the total number of people committed to participating in them.

5. Critical mass. My advice is that when planning a corporate prayer meeting, be certain you begin and continue with at least 20 people. This can be as low as 17, but no lower. When it is fewer than 17, it should properly be called and treated as small-group prayer rather than congregational corporate prayer. Group-dynamic theory, which is almost invariably borne out in practice, tells us that the *nature* of a group fewer than 17 is different from one more than 17.

Regarding maximum size, the next group-dynamic changing point is 40. Corporate prayer meetings having 35 to 50 involved will become meetings in which people will recognize each other and see few strangers. This has its advantages. But there are other advantages in a meeting of 100 or 200 or more where most of the persons can expect to be relative strangers to each other.

SEVEN GOOD REASONS FOR NOT ATTENDING CORPORATE PRAYER

A friend of mine who is the pastor of a rapidly growing church of almost 3,000 here in Southern California became excited about the Korean early-morning prayer meetings and started them in his church. He attended all of them. A healthy group of 80 people committed themselves to pray together regularly. But after a few months the 80 had dwindled to 1 or 2! What happened?

When I talked to him, we agreed that he had violated several of the following reasons for not attending corporate prayer, but it was too late. Corporate prayer has not yet been reawakened in that church because of the residual pain and discouragement all around.

If we assume that the people in the church are normal in their general spiritual life, and that they do not stay away from corporate prayer because somehow they are not right with God, here are some things to try to avoid.

"The meetings are boring." I have listed this as number one because it is number one. By far the major reason church members do not attend corporate prayer is because what happens there bores them. Few wake up in the morning thrilled with the thought that later on that evening they will be in prayer meeting.

"I have no contribution to make." Too many go to the prayer meeting as spectators, not as participants. They think that the only contribution they have personally made to the meeting is to add another body to the numbers.

"My personal needs are not met." Not only do some feel they make no contribution to others, but they also feel others make no contribution to them. Having personal needs met should not be the principal motivation for attending corporate prayer meetings, but if some do attend who have pressing personal needs, these needs should be covered in prayer sometime during or after the meeting.

"I don't know how to pray in public." People who have not learned how to join in praying out loud with others will feel ill at ease in corporate prayer over a period of time.

"The Holy Spirit doesn't show up." This is not a theological statement on God's omnipresence, but it does reflect an accurate impression, particularly on the part of those who have

degrees of spiritual discernment. If the spiritual dynamic is not strong enough to feel, what is the use of going?

"We pray, but nothing happens." If people pray, but do not see tangible answers to their prayers, they begin to feel like losers. In time, this will cause prayer meeting attendance to drop just as surely as a losing athletic team sees declining attendance at games.

"Our prayer meeting is a gossip club." I have too frequently heard someone at a prayer meeting say, "We must pray for so-and-so tonight because..." The rest of the sentence exposes something about that person's life, which, as my grandmother used to say, "should be kept within the family." This is all too often done in the flesh, not in the Spirit. A major motivation can be to communicate, "I am in the know," and the frequent result is that some of the others present perpetuate the gossip within an hour after the meeting ends under the spiritual veneer of a prayer request.

PRINCIPLES FOR POWERFUL PRAYER MEETINGS

Obviously, every one of the above reasons for not attending corporate prayer needs to be avoided. Through the experience I have personally had in leading corporate prayer, I have identified seven principles on the positive side. Because we are dealing with matters of style and not substance here, I realize that some will find my suggestions more applicable to their situation than others will.

1. Worship. The first 10 to 15 minutes of the hour should be spent in *singing* the prayers. Worship songs that address God are the most appropriate. They should be seen as a form of prayer, not as singing some songs in preparation to pray. The highest-quality worship leaders available should be in charge of this segment. One of the reasons the critical mass for corporate prayer is 20 is that with fewer than 20 people, worship in song tends to become quite anemic.

2. Verbal prayer. A few Christian traditions, such as the Quakers, attach a high value to silence in prayer. The great majority, however, from cultures around the world, prefer verbal prayer in their corporate prayer meetings. Verbal prayer falls into two general styles: concert prayer and agreement prayer.

Concert prayer (not to be confused with "concerts of prayer") means that all those present in the prayer meeting pray out loud at the same time. This is the most common form of prayer in the churches of all denominations in Korea, which, as a group, lead the world in the practice of corporate prayer. The noise level of 4,000 Koreans praying together has to be heard to be believed. And they sustain this fervent prayer for long periods of time, sometimes 20 minutes, without stopping. During that time the noise level may drop slightly, then another wave of prayer anointing comes and it picks up once again.

Concert prayer is popular among charismatics and Pentecostals in the United States and around the world. What we would call the independent charismatic movement is by far the most rapidly growing expression of Christianity in most parts of the world; thus concert prayer is or will soon become the dominant form of verbal prayer in corporate prayer meetings in general.

Agreement prayer is the kind most used in our traditional evangelical and mainline prayer meetings. One person prays out loud while the others present agree, some in more and some in less demonstrative ways.

Scripture praying, as a form of agreement prayer, is now becoming popular in many churches. In this case the pray-ers open the Bible to a passage of Scripture and partially read the text and partially pray what the Lord is showing them about the implications of the text for the actual situation. When done well, this is a moving form of prayer because it involves praying God's Word back to Him.

How to quench the Holy Spirit

In prayer meetings where verbal prayer is expected, the leader can quench the Holy Spirit in any number of ways, but three have become obvious to me:

- Allowing periods of silence. The more silence, the more people won't come back next week. Those who participate in corporate prayer can be taught to pray without ceasing, and to be alert and ready to verbalize their prayers whenever the opportunity arises. In corporate prayer, people should get used to praying many times, not just once.
- Sentence prayers or fill-in-the-blank prayers. In an effort to involve more people in the prayer meeting and to avoid periods of silence, some prayer leaders say, "Let's call out the names of God," "Let's limit our prayers to one sentence of thanksgiving to God" or "Let's all pray, 'We thank you, God because you are _____.'" Such tactics are rather wooden methods of trying to create a sense of liveliness. In the long run they will contribute to the feeling that prayer meetings are boring.
- Praying in groups of two or three. Asking those in the corporate prayer meeting to turn around and form groups of two or three to pray together definitely meets the needs of those present who are comfortable with it and have personal needs they would like others to pray for. But just as definitely it turns off others who are personally uncomfortable with the intimacy forced upon them at the moment. These will ordinarily not say anything, but they won't come back next week.

Unless the meeting is intentionally designed to serve the needs of the "groupies," it is much wiser to stay with the least common denominator and keep the large group as a large group. A compromise is to divide into groups of four to six rather than two or three. That is much less threatening to the loners, although some will still feel uncomfortable with it.

3. Mutual support. Verbal prayers should elicit verbal responses. Think of telephone manners. When one person is engaged in a monologue on the telephone, the other is expected to make sounds and speak words often enough to encourage the one who is doing the talking. The same applies to corporate prayer.

Some have criticized the Pentecostals so severely for what they consider is excessive noise; but their own prayer meetings sound like they are being held in a public library or in a morgue. Non-Pentecostals should learn good manners of verbal response in corporate prayer meetings. Pentecostals hold no copyright on "amen," "hallelujah," "thank you, Lord" or "glory to God." Granted, the loudness and the frequency will depend on the group, but in general the more and the louder the agreement is, without drowning out the pray-er, the better. Furthermore, people who experience the excitement it creates will more likely come back for prayer meeting next week.

Verbal agreement accomplishes three things:

- It encourages the pray-er.
- It gets the agree-er more involved and helps concentration.
- It builds faith and excitement in the whole group.

4. Effective prayer. As I have said before, effective prayer is defined as prayer that works. It gets answers. And effective prayer more than anything else will sustain the life and excitement of corporate prayer. Therefore, ways and means must be found to share answers to prayer in every one of the corporate prayer meetings. B. J. Willhite says, "Ordinary Christians must be convinced that their prayers make a difference. Unless a person believes that his or her prayers really make a difference, he or she is not likely to pray consistently."[7]

In church after church, I have seen prayer lists published by the church office, some of them elaborate. But in fewer than 1 out of 10 have I seen regular reports of the *answers* to these prayers. Prayer may change history, but the people who do it won't get excited about it if they do not know it is happening.

I remember hearing B. J. Willhite tell of a church he visited in Texas that had what they called a "wailing wall." On one wall of the sanctuary was a place where people would pin up photographs and file cards of unsaved people. At a given time in the service, the whole congregation would move over in front of that wall and fervently pray for the salvation of those identified on the wall.

Wonderful! Willhite asked the pastor what was happening. "They are getting saved," he responded.

Then Bob Willhite made an incredibly simple suggestion. He suggested that on the other side of the sanctuary they make a "victory wall," and in each service take photos and cards of people who are now saved off the wailing wall. They would then walk across the front of the church and pin the photos and cards on the victory wall, praying prayers of thanksgiving. This is what I mean by demonstrating effective prayer.

5. Concrete prayer. Armin Gesswein says, "General praying is never effective. There is no real faith and expectation. And prayer without faith is dead."[8] I realize it is possible that the Lord would move strongly on a given prayer meeting to do it, but usually prayer requests coming from human emotions generated by reading the headlines or hearing the news such as, "Let's pray for the families of those who lost their lives in the airplane crash in India" or "Let's pray for the South American economic summit that begins today," are far too abstract for those gathered to have any meaning at all so far as that prayer situation is concerned. Something a little closer such as, "A friend of my mother's needs prayer because her husband is threatening divorce" is more often a distraction, not a blessing.

A major problem with sentence or fill-in-the-blank prayers is that they also tend to be too abstract. The prayers we pray in a corporate prayer meeting should, to the greatest extent possible, scratch the people where they itch. Prayers need to be as concrete as possible.

6. Personalized prayer. Those who attend and participate in corporate prayer should become personally involved in the activity. A couple of suggestions:

- Train the pray-ers to use "I" instead of "we" as much as they feel comfortable doing. That draws them more directly into the prayer and allows their individuality to express itself in the group as a whole.
- Allow time in the prayer meeting when people can express urgent personal needs and have them prayed for there and then. In a one-hour meeting, the time allocated to this must be carefully controlled or it can easily turn into the kind of sharing meeting that one might expect in a small group rather than a corporate prayer meeting. But no one who comes to a corporate prayer meeting with an urgent, immediate personal need should have to go away without personal prayer.

I understand why some will say that this is the reason some prayer meetings specifically plan time for small-group prayer, and I have already pointed out the trade-offs. Another viable way of handling this is to have a prayer team remain afterward to care for personal needs. In a corporate prayer meeting of up to 50 it is feasible to designate a 10-minute slot for this and it will add positively to the dynamic of the meeting. If some of the needs are for physical healing, the laying on of hands can involve more people directly in the activities of the meeting.

    7. Practical instruction. When it comes right down to it, the way people pray in corporate prayer meetings is nothing more or less than learned behavior. Some attach their behavior, such as body language or volume, to the presence of the Holy Spirit; but the Holy Spirit does not require us to pray in any special way for Him to be present in power.

People can learn concert prayer. They can learn to verbalize agreement. They can learn to pray in paragraphs rather than in sentences. They can learn to speak promptly enough to prevent silence from deadening things. They can learn to hold their hands up or down. They can learn to share answers to prayers. They can learn to pray with eyes open or closed. They can learn good, public prayer manners.

One of the functions of schools of prayer is to teach these things to the people, especially in the beginning. Modeling and apprenticeship can help greatly. The leader can make each corporate prayer meeting a minischool of prayer by reminding the people what is expected, teaching about prayer, and encouraging those who know more than the others to demonstrate it without dominating or controlling the prayer meeting.

A hinge point in history occurred when Jesus' disciples met in agreement in prayer in the Upper Room. As a result, the Holy Spirit came on the day of Pentecost. After that, the believers were never the same, the church was never the same and the world was never the same. You also can expect to see this by using quality corporate prayer in your church.

■ REFLECTION QUESTIONS ■

1. Discuss your own feelings regarding corporate prayer. What is the state of affairs in your church?
2. List as many reasons as you can to explain why it is important for as many believers as possible to agree on what is being prayed for.
3. If the primary reason people choose not to attend church prayer meeting is that it is too boring, what can be done about this?
4. Look over the three ways to "quench the Holy Spirit" in corporate prayer meetings. Make personal comments on each of them.
5. "Concert prayer" means that everyone prays out loud at the same time. Could this work in your church? Why or why not?

Notes
1. R. A. Torrey, *How to Work for Christ* (Grand Rapids, MI: Fleming H. Revell, 1901), p. 211.
2. Sue Curran, *The Praying Church: Principles and Power of Corporate Praying* (Shekinah Publishing Company, 394 Glory Road, Blountville, TN 37617).
3. Alvin Vander Griend, *The Praying Church Sourcebook* (Grand Rapids, MI: Church Development Resources, 1990).
4. Curran, *The Praying Church*, pp. 27,28.
5. Frances Smyth, "Prayer Ministry," *The Alamo City Reflections*, September 25, 1991, p. 4.
6. Curran, *The Praying Church*, p. 48.
7. B. J. Willhite, "How to Get Your People to Pray," *Ministries Today*, November-December, 1988, p. 36.
8. Armin Gesswein, "Churches on Fire!" *Alliance Life*, n.d.

Prayer Can Change Your Community

WE ARE HALFWAY THROUGH THE BOOK, AND IT IS TIME for a midcourse assessment. So far, I have attempted to do three things:

- The first chapter described the exciting prayer movement that is sweeping the world in which many of us desire to participate.
- Two chapters probed deeply into the nature of prayer, both in speaking to God and in hearing from God.
- Two further chapters explained how prayer can be a vital and life-giving part of the week-in and week-out activities of your local church.

Now I want to shift the focus of prayer and move outside of the local church and into the community. Much of what I will be sharing in the rest of the book will be relatively new. The Holy Spirit has been showing things to the people of God in the 1990s that all but a very few were aware of in the 1980s.

REVIVAL IS COMING

There is an awesome feel about what is now going on. No one in my generation has experienced true worldwide revival, so we can only imagine what it might feel like. My sense is that most of us alive now will live to see the great revival. I cannot set dates, but it does seem as if this is the generation that will experience the greatest outpouring of the Holy Spirit perhaps in all of history.

The conditions that have preceded revivals in past history seem to be coming together. One by one they are fitting like pieces in a giant picture puzzle in which the image of revival is becoming clearer and clearer. I think the holiness movement of more than 100 years ago may have been the seed; from it, in the early years of our century, came the Pentecostal movement.

After World War II, the great global harvest of souls began, which has increased ever since. God began impressing the Church with a greater burden for the poor and oppressed, highlighting our social responsibilities, in the 1960s. This continues to grow. Then came the great prayer movement, which I have been describing in this book, and also the resurgence of the modern prophetic movement. As we entered the 1990s, spiritual warfare began to rise high on the agendas of active Christians.

Added to this is extreme moral and social degradation. Neo-Nazi racists are surfacing in Germany. High-rolling financiers are accused of defrauding the American public through savings and loans. Defenseless, unborn babies are ruthlessly slaughtered by the millions with no feelings of guilt or remorse. Vast amounts of natural resources are being exploited to satisfy human greed. AIDS is decimating entire nations in Africa and elsewhere. Whole peoples are dedicated to slaughtering each other in the Balkans, the Middle East and Southeast Asia. All around us we see those who are filled with unrighteousness, sexual immorality, covetousness, envy, murder, deceit; they are haters of God, violent, disobedient to parents, unloving and unforgiving, just to select a few signs of moral and social decay from Romans 1:29-31.

This should not surprise us. History shows that parallel to the increase in the power of God preceding a revival comes a corresponding increase in public and corporate sin. In the Old Testament, it happened before the revival under Samuel, the revival under David and the revival under Hezekiah just to name a few. Presidents will lie. Congresses will pass laws condoning immorality. Supreme Courts will issue ungodly interpretations of constitutions. Social analysts will proclaim that we are entering a post-Christian era.

All that would be overwhelming if we did not also know that after God's judgment, He will pour out His mighty power!

THE GREAT HARVEST

Worldwide we are witnessing what, by any standard of measurement, is the greatest ingathering of souls since the time of Jesus. Although no one can give exact statistics, those who are well informed on China tell us that possibly 35,000 persons *a day* are becoming Christians, up from 20,000 during parts of the 1980s. And this in a nation where every form of political and military coercion has been used for 40 years to wipe out Christianity. In Africa, south of the Sahara, it is estimated that some 20,000 to 30,000 are turning to Christ every day. One denomination in South Africa holds annual Easter conventions, which draw a reported 2 million believers together each time.

Someone calculated that in Latin America 400 people are

born again each hour around the clock. Guatemala now numbers more than 30 percent evangelicals and has elected a committed, evangelical Christian as president. A church that meets in a theater in downtown Buenos Aires, Argentina, now holds services 23 hours a day, 7 days a week. They close from 12:00 midnight to 1:00 A.M. for cleaning. The Pope has become so alarmed with the increasing number of born-again evangelicals in Latin America that he has pushed the panic button and commanded it to be stopped.

The fall of the Iron Curtain has produced a historic phenomenon in Eastern Europe. Never before have such a large number of people turned from being staunchly resistant to the gospel to enthusiastically receptive to the gospel in such a short time period. A friend of mine, who is not particularly known as an evangelist, recently visited a small city in the Ukraine, which had no Christian presence. When he arrived, he was asked to speak in the local hockey stadium and explain Christianity to the people. The people were so hungry to hear that they got into physical brawls, first over empty seats, then over free Russian New Testaments that were being distributed.

He preached a salvation message through an interpreter and gave an invitation. All 4,000 attendees stood to their feet to accept Jesus Christ. Thinking they were insincere or did not understand, he repeated the invitation and had the same results. A Russian friend then told him that these people were dead serious. Some had left their farms at a crucial time in the harvest season to attend. They had decided they wanted to be Christians before they came and they only needed to know how to do it!

I have received so many reports containing similar drama and magnitude that I have lost count.

Pushing Back the Devil

I have seen no one describing it better than George Otis Jr., in his remarkable book *The Last of the Giants.* If we might tend to be discouraged about the worldwide spread of the gospel, we but need to take a bird's-eye view of what has happened over the last 2,000 years.

"In the days of the early church," Otis says, "mission strategy was relatively simple. *All* lands were unevangelized, *all* peoples were unreached." Through the next 1,900 years the tide ebbed and flowed, but the net result was advance, first through the Roman Empire, then through Europe and to the Americas and Australia. Otis says, "Up to this point, from a satanic perspective, things had not gone altogether badly...Christianity was still fairly contained."

But, again from Satan's perspective, "What was *not* expected, and certainly much less welcomed, was the disastrous eruption of global evangelization in the twentieth century." As a result, "Much to the dismay of the enemy, the borders of the unevangelized world have been heaved backward so forcefully that 75 percent of the world's population now have a reasonable opportunity to hear the Gospel."

"10/40 WINDOW"

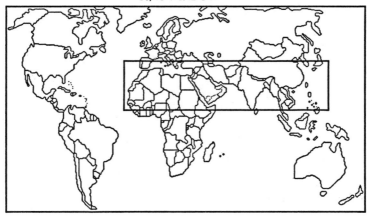

The current state of affairs, according to Otis, is that the armies of God "have now encircled the final strongholds of the serpent—the nations and spiritual principalities of the 10/40 Window. While the remaining task is admittedly the most challenging phase of the battle, the armies of Lucifer are faced presently with a community of believers whose spiritual resources—if properly motivated, submitted, and unified—are truly awesome."[1]

Jesus Says Pray

Jesus makes a very significant and well-known statement about the harvest: "The harvest truly is plentiful, but the laborers are few" (Matt. 9:37). This situation is commonplace among farmers. The one time during the agricultural cycle that most workers are needed is at harvesttime. As farmers know, if not enough workers are on hand at harvesttime, the harvest will pass and the crop will be lost.

But Jesus was making an evangelistic application, speaking of multitudes, who, without God, are as sheep without a shepherd. We have such a harvest on our hands today—multitudes without God who are ready to receive the gospel. And the laborers are all too few.

What are we to do then? Many forms of action need to be taken, but the very first one Jesus mentions is to *pray*. "Pray the Lord of the harvest," He says, "to send out laborers into His harvest" (Matt. 9:38). The implications of this seem clear for us today. Suppose we decide not to pray? Obviously a great deal of the harvest will then be lost. I am again reminded of what Jack Hayford said, "If we don't, He won't." In some theological as well as practical sense, God's desire that all be saved will either be fulfilled or unfulfilled depending on our prayers.

EVANGELIZATION IS SPIRITUAL WARFARE

The principal target for world evangelization in the 1990s might be the 10/40 Window, but to be honest most of us feel more responsibility for our own community here at home. Although we want to be involved in world missions and some of us would be open to the personal call of God to move cross-culturally, that is not where we are living at the moment. If I look up and down my own block, I see plenty of sheep without a shepherd. How can they be won to Christ?

The settings may be different, but the principles are the same. Why would Jesus say that our first responsibility for penetrating our community with the gospel is to pray? It is because He knew what many of us tend to ignore: Evangelization whether in the 10/40 Window or on my block is *spiritual warfare.*

If we are unclear about this, we need only to think back on the conversion of the apostle Paul. Then known as Saul of Tarsus, he was one of the fiercest and most feared enemies of Christianity. But on his way to Damascus, where he was going to persecute Christians, Saul was dramatically converted by a personal appearance of Jesus. Not only was he born again, but Jesus called him to world evangelization at the same time. And He gave Paul clear instructions.

When Paul, in obedience to the Lord, would arrive in a given nation he would naturally find a population of unbelievers. His God-given job description was specific. He was to turn those people "from darkness to light, and from the power of Satan to God" (Acts 26:18). What Paul may not have known then, but later learned through experience, was that when Satan has unbelievers under his control, he does not give them up without a fight This is what we now call spiritual warfare.

Our Principal Weapon Is Prayer

When I say Paul later learned this, I think of what he wrote to the believers in Ephesus. "For we do not wrestle against flesh and blood, but against principalities, against powers, against the rulers of the darkness of this age, against spiritual hosts of wickedness in the heavenly places" (Eph. 6:12). This is known as one of the chief passages in the New Testament on spiritual warfare.

A good bit of what Paul writes here is a description of the

Without a weapon as powerful as prayer we could not hope to take people from under the power of Satan,...and bring them to faith in Jesus Christ.

---

armament and weaponry we are issued by God to engage the enemy in spiritual warfare. I like the way New Testament scholar, Clinton E. Arnold, explains this passage. He points out that, although for Paul spiritual warfare is both defensive and offensive, it "is more proactive than reactive."[2] As Arnold paraphrases Paul, "The primary aggressive action the Christian is called to take in the world is to spread the gospel."[3]

Having said that, what is the principal weapon of spiritual warfare that we need when we move into the evangelization of our community? Prayer! Arnold says, "If Paul were to summarize the primary way of gaining access to the power of God for waging successful spiritual warfare, he would unwaveringly affirm that it is through prayer. Prayer is given much greater prominence in the spiritual warfare passage than any of the other implements."[4]

Now it may be somewhat clearer why Jesus would say that when we find ourselves in the midst of a great harvest with too few laborers, we should pray. Without a weapon as powerful as prayer we could not hope to take people from under the power of Satan, whom Paul calls, "the god of this age" (2 Cor. 4:4) and bring them to faith in Jesus Christ. Without prayer we would be rendered virtually impotent in trying to evangelize either our own city or the 10/40 Window.

WARFARE PRAYER

Once we understand why prayer is important for reaching our community for Christ, we then must decide what kind of prayer we will use. As I have mentioned previously, many kinds of prayer are used in the Bible. All of them are important and each is appropriate for certain circumstances.

The type of prayer most indicated for evangelism designed to take unbelievers from darkness to light and from the power of Satan to God is warfare prayer. It is otherwise known as "binding the strongman." Another book in this *Prayer Warrior* series, *Warfare Prayer* (Regal Books), goes into this subject in great detail. At this point, we simply need to be clear about what the Bible means by "binding the strongman."

A milestone in Jesus' earthly ministry came when Peter, on behalf of all the disciples, declared, "You are the Christ, the Son of the living God" (Matt. 16:16). In response, Jesus for the first time told them why He had come: "I will build My church" (Matt. 16:18). Building the Church, of course, is an evangelistic statement.

Then Jesus adds, "The gates of Hades shall not prevail against it." Here is a strong hint of the spiritual warfare awaiting anyone attempting to build the Church. Satan does not intend to allow it to go unopposed. But Satan will not be able to stop the forward advance of the gospel because Jesus said, "I will give you the keys of the kingdom of heaven" (Matt. 16:19). God's Kingdom will advance if those keys are used.

But, what are the keys?

Jesus said, "Whatever you bind on earth will be bound in heaven, and whatever you loose on earth will be loosed in heaven" (Matt. 16:19). Binding, then, has evangelistic significance. Now the disciples were beginning to understand more about what Jesus meant when He previously said to them, "How can one enter a strong man's house and plunder his goods, unless he first *binds* the strong man?" (Matt. 12:29, emphasis mine).

Taking the Armor and Dividing the Spoils

Jesus' clearest teaching on the strongman is found in Luke 11. This is a passage on demons, which begins in Luke 11:14; Jesus is casting out a demon from a mute man. When the demon left, the man spoke for the first time.

The Pharisees were watching this dramatic demonstration of supernatural power, and asking themselves, "How did He do it?" Their conclusion was logical, given their own assumptions. They said, "He casts out demons by Beelzebub, the ruler of the demons" (Luke 14:15). Notice that they escalated the scenario.

In *Warfare Prayer,* I distinguish between ground-level spiritual warfare, occult-level spiritual warfare and strategic-level spiritual warfare. Jesus started on ground level by casting out an ordinary demon, but the Pharisees escalated it to strategic level by mentioning Beelzebub, one of the chief principalities. So the rest of this passage deals with strategic-level warfare, the kind that calls for warfare prayer.

Jesus, of course, denies that He cast out demons by the power of Beelzebub, but rather by "the finger of God," (Luke 11:20) which, as we see in the parallel passage in Matthew 12:28, means "the Spirit of God." The source of Jesus' power was the Kingdom of light, not the kingdom of darkness.

Jesus then uses the occasion for some significant teaching.

He says, "When a strong man, fully armed, guards his own palace, his goods are in peace" (Luke 11:21). Obviously, in this context the "strong man" refers to Beelzebub or some other high-ranking principality. What are the "goods" that principalities and powers of darkness guard so jealously? Undoubtedly there are many, but none more valuable to them than unsaved souls. So long as the strong man's armor is intact, he has the unsaved souls where he wants them.

But when a "stronger than he," which could mean only the Holy Spirit, "overcomes him" or as Matthew would say, "binds him," "he takes from him all his armor in which he trusted, and divides his spoils" (Luke 11:22). What activates this spiritual warfare done to bind principalities and powers? As we saw from Ephesians 6, it is prayer, specifically warfare prayer.

In summary, binding the strongman is using the keys of the Kingdom of heaven so that the gates of Hades will not obstruct building Christ's Church here on earth. Through warfare prayer, we can free unsaved souls and take them "from darkness to light, and from the power of Satan to God" (Acts 26:18).

We must also keep in mind that binding the strongman is not evangelism. It never saved anyone. Only the gospel of Jesus Christ is the power of God for salvation as Paul says in Romans 1:16. We preach Christ and Him crucified. But there are multitudes in our world and in our own communities who, if things do not change, will never be able to hear the gospel of Christ and make a decision to accept Him or reject Him. I believe that Spirit-led warfare prayer can change things and help remove the blinders that the god of this age has attached.

Praying *for* the Community

How is significant prayer for our communities to be translated into action today? God is answering this question in remarkable ways and providing us the means to pray as we never have before.

Christians pray for their communities in two major ways:

- Prayer in the local church carried on by the church members.
- Christian people from many local churches praying together for their community.

If we were to analyze the prayer life of most local churches today, we would find little overt, explicit prayer for the community. Many churches do pray for unsaved people in their community, but they do not pray much for the community as a whole. This is partly because the needs of the congregation are

---

The thing the territorial spirits fear the most is the unity of pastors, and through them the unity of the Body of Christ.

---

so great that they themselves require much prayer time. But partly it may be because of discouragement. When they have previously tried to pray for their community, they have not seen much change.

One of the reasons for this is that the authority of one local church is not too great in the community as a whole. The more we are learning about "taking our cities for God"[5] as John Dawson might say, the more we are understanding the literal meaning of Jesus' prayer in John 17: "That they also may be one in Us, that the world may believe that You sent Me" (John 17:21). Without the visible, practical unity of the Body of Christ in a given city, few answers to even the most fervent warfare prayer can be expected.

The unity necessary in a given city for effective spiritual warfare must begin with unity among pastors and top Christian leaders. The pastors of the local churches are the spiritual gatekeepers of the city, and as such they have divine authority. Apparently Satan knows much better than many pastors that, "by uniting we stand; by dividing we fall" (John Dickinson, 1768). In city after city, Satan has succeeded in keeping pastors divided and thus maintained the authority of whatever strongman he has assigned to the city. For good reason, the thing these territorial spirits fear the most is the unity of pastors, and through them the unity of the Body of Christ.

Concerts of Prayer

One of the first to recognize the lack of united prayer and who began to take steps to change the situation was David Bryant, founder of Concerts of Prayer International. Throughout the 1980s, my friend David rose to the top across America as a chief promoter of citywide united prayer. Although relatively few leaders were talking about it then, Bryant's zeal never flagged.

Bryant was greatly inspired by Jonathan Edwards' leadership in America's First Great Awakening and the book Edwards wrote to prepare Christians for it: *An Humble Attempt to Promote Explicit Agreement and Visible Union of God's People in Extraordinary Prayer of the Revival of Religion and the Advancement of Christ's Kingdom on Earth*. Bryant regards that rather lengthy title as a definition of "concerts of prayer."[6]

In developing the concerts of prayer, Bryant was attempting to combine the strengths of the two types of prayer groups he had observed: those that prayed for revival in the church, and those that prayed for outreach. He recognized that inward prayer must be balanced with outward prayer for the community and the world.

Jonathan Edwards's vision of "visible union of God's people" is seen as a key ingredient for concerts of prayer. Bryant says, "A concert of prayer provides a visible expression of the unity in the Body of Christ." He sees it as an answer to Christ's prayer in John 17, and adds, "Through corporate intercession we are newly forged to Christ, to each other and to Christ's mission in the world."[7]

As concerts of prayer have multiplied in cities through the United States and Canada, significant advances have been made in uniting Christian people in prayer for their communities. Again, the more local church pastors have caught the vision of concerts of prayer and personally participated, the stronger they have been.

Prayer Summits

Perhaps through understanding the need for pastors to take the lead in bringing forth the unity of the Body of Christ in a city, Joe Aldrich has launched prayer summits, which he defines as "conferences designed to bring about renewal and unity among pastors and other church leaders."[8]

Beginning in the Northwest, where Aldrich serves as president of Multnomah School of the Bible in Portland, Oregon, he and those he is training have conducted prayer summits in city after city. The results, which have come to be almost predictable, are remarkable. This seems to me to be an example of a concept that is enjoying a powerful, divine anointing for the kinds of things God desires to accomplish among the spiritual leaders or gatekeepers of our cities today.

Prayer summits have great potential to begin the process of radical change in the spiritual atmosphere of our cities. Indeed, the subtitle of Aldrich's book *Prayer Summits* is: *Seeking God's Agenda for Your Community*. A unique feature of a prayer summit is that pastors get together in a retreat setting for 4 days and have no agenda of their own whatsoever. They have no lineup of speakers and no daily program. They usually end up singing 75 to 100 songs and hymns a day, pray together, listen to God, read Scripture and receive whatever the Holy Spirit might have for them. One of the normal ministries of the Holy Spirit is deep repentance and forgiveness. Leaders are permanently bonded together for whatever else God might have for their community.

Pastors who attend a prayer summit are encouraged to hold solemn assemblies in their churches. Solemn assemblies are "specially called assemblies designed to address disobedience and sin in the congregation of a local church."[9]

Following a prayer summit and several solemn assemblies, the pastors of Portland, Oregon, decided to cancel their Sunday night church services and meet in the Portland Coliseum in early 1992. About 13,500 from all churches and all traditions showed up for what was described as, "The best family reunion Portland has ever had." Dale German, a Nazarene pastor, reports, "The celebrating never let up. Together we sang and prayed and clapped for God. All of us share the burden. All of us feel the spiritual oppression in Portland and the Northwest. All of us want to have the city of Portland shaken for God and righteousness."[10]

City Prayer Alerts

Although it has not been widely tested at this writing, one of the most promising concepts for citywide united prayer has emerged from Avery Willis of the Southern Baptist Sunday School Board. Under the A.D. 2000 United Prayer Track, he is developing materials to help organize prayer groups from the churches in a given city to furnish a 24-hour-a-day prayer blanket for the community.

Each prayer group signs up for 1 hour a week, which means

a total of 168 prayer groups are needed to cover each city. The design is simple: When each group is about to conclude their hour's prayer, they telephone the next group to make sure that the chain does not stop. This has the potential of linking the citywide Body of Christ for a week-in-week-out community prayer effort that has no precedent I know of. Along with concerts of prayer and prayer summits, it can pave the way for permanent change in the atmosphere of the city.

PRAYING *IN* THE COMMUNITY

In the decade of the 1990s, God has been surfacing a concept, which, at least for me, is invigoratingly new. A few have been practicing it for a while, but now God is showing the whole Body of Christ how to pray *in* the community.

Concerts of prayer, prayer summits, city prayer alerts and many other similar activities are designed to promote prayer *for* the city. I belong to a movement called "Love L.A." The pastors gather three times a year from 7:00 A.M. to 11:00 A.M. for united prayer in Hollywood Presbyterian Church and then one night a year in South Central Los Angeles at Crenshaw Christian Center, where all church members are invited. From 400 to 1,200 pastors attend, and up to 8,000 lay people gather for prayer. In Love L.A. we pray *for* our city.

For some time, I had been feeling in my spirit that God was trying to show us something new. Not that the old was bad or that it should be phased out. Quite the contrary, our prayers for the city need to be multiplied in frequency and intensity. It is not either/or, it is both/and. I agree with what I heard David Bryant say in the North American Conference on Strategic-Level Prayer in 1993: "Strategic-level praying must never be carried out apart from uniting in revival praying, *because* to the degree God wins the battle on the inside of the Church and removes the strongholds there; to that degree will all other prayer for the 10/40 Window ultimately prevail."

Getting the Walls Down

Uniting in revival praying is so important to me that I shall not soon forget a church growth conference in Second Baptist Church of Houston I attended in the spring of 1992 where I heard Jack Graham, pastor of Prestonwood Baptist Church of Dallas, verbalize exactly what I sensed God had been showing me:

Revival will come when we get the walls down between the church and the community.

I was deeply stirred in my spirit when I heard that. It has become what I believe to be a prophetic word for me personally and for the Body of Christ as a whole. Much of what God desires to do in our cities in the 1990s will happen if we obey this word, and conversely much of what God desires will *not* happen if we fail to obey.

I love the way Jack Graham said it. "*Revival will come...*" Revival only comes. We do not produce or generate it. God sends revival by His Holy Spirit.

But there is a condition: "*when we get the walls down between the church and the community.*" God is not going to bring those walls down Himself. He could do so by His sovereign power, but He has chosen not to. I imagine one of the reasons might be that He did not put them up in the first place. It is up to us to get those walls down.

Of all the churches of all denominations in London, England, the one that has made the most measurable impact on its immediate community is Kensington Temple, according to a recent study by MARC Europe. Pastor Wynne Lewis has revealed that in 1982, 26 witches' covens were located within a kilometer radius of the church. They had joined forces and declared, "We are going to close Kensington Temple down."

Hearing this, a woman from Uganda who was a member of the congregation approached Pastor Lewis with a look of indignation and disdain. She said, "Who are the witches who want to close us down? Find their addresses and give them to me!" She formed a prayer team with intercessors from Ghana and Nigeria and went into the community, holding warfare prayer meetings outside the witches' centers. One by one they closed down. These African women knew how to get the walls down.[11]

As an aside, some will notice that this book on prayer relating to the local church is the fourth in the *Prayer Warrior* series. When I designed the series, I thought this book might be the first. But month after month, I could not get started on this book although I had all the material I needed. Then God showed me why. He told me in His way that I was working on only half the proper assumption. My idea was to do a book on prayer in the local church, part of which would be prayer *for the community*. The missing half, God showed me, was prayer outside the walls of the church *in the community*. The last four chapters comprise what formerly was the missing half.

BOTH TO WILL AND TO DO

Not only has God told us to move our prayers into the community, but He has also given us some exciting and innovative ways to do it. Furthermore, they are fun! Prayer that is fun is a fairly unusual concept, but I believe God is fulfilling for us what Paul wrote to the Philippians: "For it is God who works in you both *to will* and to do for His good pleasure" (Phil. 2:13, emphasis mine).

Four ways of praying in the community have surfaced as principal Christian activities for the 1990s. More may be forthcoming, but these are now in place:

- **Praise Marches.** These are focused on cities.

- **Prayerwalks.** These are focused on neighborhoods.
- **Prayer Expeditions.** These are focused on regions.
- **Prayer Journeys.** These are focused on strongholds.

A Scripture reference that I sense is a prophetic word for praying outside of our churches today is Joshua 1:3, given by God to Joshua as he was preparing to lead the people of God into the Promised Land. God said: *"Every place that the sole of your foot will tread upon I have given you"* (emphasis mine). I believe God is nudging us outside of our churches through our concerts of prayer or our prayer summits and into our communities to physically pray there.

As we obey Him, we will be getting nearer and nearer to the revival He desires to send.

▬ REFLECTION QUESTIONS ▬

1. Do you agree that the Church worldwide is on the threshold of the great revival? What are some of the things that lead you to your conclusion?
2. Look back at the map of the "10/40 Window." Name some of the countries there and share what you believe are important prayer needs in those countries.
3. In what ways is it accurate to say that evangelism is spiritual warfare? Does "binding the strongman" save souls by itself? Talk about this.
4. Discuss the benefits of concerts of prayer and prayer summits. Have you experienced either or have you heard reports from others about them? Do you think it would be possible to hold a regular concert of prayer in your city? If so, call or write: Concerts of Prayer International, P.O. Box 36008, Minneapolis, MN 55435, Tel: 612-853-1740, Fax: 612-853-8474.

5. How would you yourself verbalize the crucial difference between praying *for* your community and praying *in* your community? Do you agree that Joshua 1:3 could have a direct application today?

Notes

1. George Otis Jr., *The Last of the Giants* (Grand Rapids, MI: Chosen Books, 1991), pp. 143,144.
2. Clinton E. Arnold, *Powers of Darkness* (Downers Grove, IL: InterVarsity Press, 1992), p. 159.
3. Ibid., p. 157.
4. Ibid., p. 158.
5. John Dawson, *Taking Our Cities for God* (Lake Mary, FL: Creation House, 1989).
6. David Bryant, *How Christians Can Join Together in Concerts of Prayer for Spiritual Awakening and World Evangelization* (Ventura, CA: Regal Books, 1988), p. 13.
7. Ibid., p. 96.
8. Joe Aldrich, *Prayer Summits* (Portland, OR: Multnomah Press, 1992), p. 15.
9. Ibid.
10. Ibid.
11. Wynne Lewis, "The Supernatural," *World Pentecost,* Spring 1993, p. 5.

Praise Marches

I N THE FALL OF 1991, DORIS AND I WERE IN NÜRNBERG, Germany. Nürnberg, among other things, was one of the central locations of Adolf Hitler's Nazi power. Here the troops would pass in review and Hitler would boast to the world of his military might. Nürnberg was one of the sites of the notorious nationwide "crystal night" on November 9, 1938, when Hitler began his ruthless slaughter of more than 6 million Jews.

THE BERLIN DECLARATION

I had been invited as a keynote speaker for a church growth conference jointly sponsored by the German Church Growth Society and the Renewal Movement of the Protestant State Church. The former were largely noncharismatics and the latter charismatics. This in itself was remarkable because Germany has been known as one of the nations of the world having the highest wall separating charismatics and noncharismatics. About 5,000 attended the conference and the leaders of both groups shared equally from the platform.

Historically, a major barrier to Christian unity in Germany was erected by the leaders of the Pietist Movement and the Evangelical Alliance in 1909 with what they called "The Berlin Declaration." This was one of the strongest anticharismatic statements ever issued, attributing the activities of charismatics (or Pentecostals) to power coming "from below," not from above. And periodically through the years those claiming to be pietists had reaffirmed their adherence to The Berlin Declaration. It had become a true stronghold of the enemy to keep the Body of Christ fragmented.

A March in Nürnberg

Soon after we arrived, we were told that the organizers of the conference had planned a March for Jesus through the streets of Nürnberg on one of the days of the conference. It was to begin and end right in the open marketplace where Hitler had staged his "crystal night." The day of the march was a cold, rainy day. Nevertheless, around 8,500 people showed up holding banners, balloons, decorated umbrellas and they were in a joyous, festive mood. Vans had been fitted with speakers and a platform had been erected for the prayer meeting at the end of the march.

The march wound through the central city streets of Nürnberg for about 2 miles. The believers of the city had come together to sing praises to God in unison. Doris and I joined the march; Doris was pushed in a wheelchair because of a deteriorated knee, which later required surgical replacement. We were both overwhelmed with emotion. For the first 10 minutes, we could neither talk nor sing. We were weeping under the presence of the Holy Spirit who was giving us a glimpse of the incredible spiritual victories being won over the forces of darkness in the invisible world.

One of the conference leaders approached me. He was obviously feeling what we were feeling as well. He said, "We have decided to change our program tonight. We need to do public repentance. And we would also like you to change your message and speak on repentance."

That evening the Holy Spirit was powerfully at work. I told of the prophecy of the threefold cord not easily broken, which I have mentioned in a previous chapter. I told of the Lausanne Congress in Manila, where charismatics and noncharismatics were joined by God's Spirit as two of the cords for world evangelization. I was also bold enough to admit the disappointment on the part of those of us who were leaders of the Manila Congress when the German delegates publicly protested that the ministry of Jack Hayford in a plenary session was too charismatic, and offensive to them. They implied that it was probably offensive to God as well.

I concluded by recounting an incident in Tokyo in 1990 in which God led me into public repentance. As an American, I humbled myself before about 1,000 Japanese leaders and repented of the sin of dropping the atomic bomb on Hiroshima and Nagasaki in World War II. Following that, Japanese pastors took the microphone and repented, using great emotion, for the sins Japan had committed not only against America but against many other nations as well.

Repudiating The Berlin Declaration
By the time I finished speaking, the Holy Spirit had come powerfully over the audience at Nürnberg. Many of the 5,000 attendees were audibly weeping. Then the leader of the noncharismatic faction, Klaus Eickhoff, took the platform and, using a magnificent combination of eloquence and remorse, declared that The Berlin Declaration was null and void and confessed

that in propagating it they had sinned not only against God but also against Martin Luther's own teachings.

The charismatic leader, Friedrich Aschoff, responded by speaking appropriate words of forgiveness and counter repentance for spiritual arrogance and pride. The conference received wide publicity in the German media, some of it negative, from theologians who yet affirmed The Berlin Declaration. But for many, the meeting was a historic turning point for the unity of the Body of Christ in Germany.

Why do I tell this story?

As a firsthand observer, I believe that one of the key visible instruments God used to bring repentance and unity was the March for Jesus. The spiritual power released in that Nürnberg praise march was awesome.

THE CHURCH IN THE STREETS

March for Jesus was pioneered by Graham Kendrick, a young British songwriter and worship leader; Roger Forster, founder of the Ichthus Christian Fellowship; Gerald Coates, founder of Pioneer Ministries; and Lynn Green of YWAM. An "embryonic, improvised march," to use Graham Kendrick's words[1], through the notorious Soho district of London in 1985 started the creative juices of these four somewhat iconoclastic innovators churning.

What they clearly saw is colorfully summarized by Graham Kendrick: "So much of what happens in the church goes on behind closed doors. The once powerful, visible church has become virtually invisible. I have a vision for the church becoming visible again—the 'bride on display' if you will. It's time for the bride of Christ to quit hiding and show herself."[2] This is another way of saying that the Church not only should pray *for* the community, but also should pray *in* the community.

The first March for Jesus was announced for May 1987 in

London. The organizers hoped that up to 5,000 might show up to proclaim their faith. When it turned out to be a miserable, rainy day they mentally downscaled their expectations. But a surprising 15,000 joined in the march and the feedback was tremendously positive. They knew they had a winner.

The next year the London March for Jesus drew no fewer than 55,000. In 1989, they decided to decentralize it and marches were organized in 45 large cities. In 1990, in 700 cities and towns on the same day throughout the U.K. an estimated 200,000 marched. In 1991, there was a similar turnout. That year also, Tom Pelton organized the first United States citywide March for Jesus in Austin, Texas, where 15,000 Christians from 120 churches joined in public praise. Spontaneous marches were also held in Argentina, Japan, Zimbabwe, Guatemala, Brazil, Australia and, as I have described, Nürnberg, Germany.

A Day to Change the World

In May 1992, the first coordinated international March for Jesus, initially planned for Europe, spread across the Atlantic to the United States as well. This was to be a forerunner of international marches in June 1993, then what is being called "A Day to Change the World" on June 25, 1994. This massive prayer initiative, coordinated by the A.D. 2000 United Prayer Track, has programmed numerous large-scale prayer events for that day sponsored by virtually all of the existing international Christian prayer networks.

It is anticipated that up to 30 percent of the world's committed Christians will participate on June 25, 1994, in synchronized, coordinated, informed prayer for their own communities and nations and for the peoples of the 10/40 Window. The centerpiece of the day will be Marches for Jesus in almost every capital city of almost every nation in the world, including many hundreds of other cities. The A.D. 2000 committee of Seoul,

Korea, has set a goal of 2 million Korean Christians participating that day in the city of Seoul alone.

If May 23, 1992, is any indicator, there is great hope. On that day, the March for Jesus unfolded in 200 cities, 40 in Europe and 160 in the United States and Canada. More than 600,000 participated. The marches were all different, yet they were all the same.

Here is how Graham Kendrick describes one of the Marches for Jesus: "A forest of banners rose and began to move like a living thing, as slowly the great procession got underway. Children riding in strollers or on shoulders; the disabled rolling by in their wheelchairs; people of every age, color and class linking arms. Here and there the more agile broke into impromptu ring dances, as musicians attempted to walk and play at once. Our hearts melted together as everyone's preoccupation became giving glory to God."[3]

Jesus Is Alive and Well

In city after city on May 23, 1992, believers were encouraged in their faith and witness, new levels of Christian unity were achieved and onlookers discovered that the Church of Jesus Christ was alive and well in their communities. Here are some of the firsthand reports:

Erica Youngman of London, England: "A colorful crowd of over 45,000 marched for Jesus from Battersea Park to Hyde Park in London. The atmosphere was even more joyful than previous marches, with Christians from the entire spectrum of denominations involved, including many from the West Indian churches. There was positive coverage on both of our national television networks—a breakthrough!"

Lynne Quanrud of Tirana, Albania: "The march started with 300, but had swelled to over 2,000 by the end. People appreciated the freedom of being able to have the march, and there was a real sense of blessing on the nation."

Tobias Gerster of Berlin, Germany: "Together, despite all denominational differences, 60,000 walked the streets publicly confessing their faith. With the sun shining they marched through the Brandenburg Gate, the symbol of the separation of Germany through Communist influence. The march was an impressive sign of the change in Germany."

Tom Pelton of Austin, Texas: "A conservative estimate of the participation this year is 20,000. For six days preceding the march we were engulfed with torrential rain. On the day of the march we had blue skies and temperatures in the 80s. An offering of $20,000 was received and given entirely to the City of Austin for the Children's Hospital."

Dougie Brown of Moscow, Russia: "500 marchers left the rallying point 2 miles from the Kremlin and marched with colorful banners, ribbons, and flags proclaiming Jesus. There was tremendous worship outside Gorky Park and another 100 joined the group. About 15 people were saved."

Garry Martin of Memphis, Tennessee: "In this city, known for racial segregation, a white pastor and a black pastor worked together as organizers. The location they chose was the place where blacks had been auctioned as slaves more than one hundred years ago. The march was 50/50 black and white, a powerful public testimony of the love of Jesus."

Zdzislaw Weyna of Wroclaw, Poland: "4,500 people took part in the march in Wroclaw, coming into the city from different regions of the nation. Many remarked about the magnificent atmosphere of prayer and good cooperation of the city administration. We saw walls of mistrust crumble between leaders and believers of the different denominations. The believers are now joyfully awaiting the next march."

Add to these similar testimonies from participants in 193 other cities, and the impact of these public praise marches will begin to come clear.

ARE PRAISE MARCHES PRAYER?

Some will undoubtedly be wondering why I am including a chapter on praise marches in a book on prayer. For many of us, prayer means talking to God in our daily devotional time, bowing our heads to say grace at the table or closing our eyes while the pastor leads in prayer in a church service. The proper posture for prayer is "heads bowed and eyes closed," as we are used to hearing Billy Graham say.

How, then, could walking through the streets with our eyes open, clapping hands, waving banners, singing and shouting, playing tambourines and dancing be even remotely considered as prayer?

Although it takes awhile for some of us to get used to this particular form of praise as legitimate prayer, we have never really doubted that praise, in and by itself, is a part of prayer. When the disciples asked Jesus to teach them to pray, Jesus responded with what we call the Lord's Prayer. And it begins, "Our Father who art in heaven, hallowed be Thy name" (Matt. 6:9, *NASB*). Sometimes the archaic word "hallowed" masks what this really means. *The Living Bible* puts it in plainer language: "we honor your holy name." Giving honor, worship and praise to God *is* prayer.

A technical distinction exists between worship and praise, but it is not something we rigidly press. Worship is expressing our deep love and devotion to God. Praise is declaring back to God, to ourselves, and to the world the greatness, majesty, power and glory of God. In daily language, however, worship and praise are used with considerable overlap in meaning. In our worship times, we also praise and in our praise times we also worship. "Hallowed be thy name" can be stretched to include them both.

How this praise and worship is expressed in a given time and place is a matter of form, not of substance. When something good happens, we can say "Praise the Lord!" We can begin our church services having someone leading the congregation in a "prayer of praise." To raise the noise level we can all stand and join the choir and organ in singing "Holy, Holy, Holy."

Different churches do it different ways. Some say, "Let's give Jesus a hand!" and the response is a thunderous applause, including some cheering and whistling. Some praise with their hands down, some with their hands up. Some have extended periods of worship singing, using contemporary choruses. Others sing less, using more traditional hymns and looking to choirs and soloists to do much of their praise singing for them.

THE POWER OF PRAISE

Whatever the form, praise pleases God, it draws us near to Him (see Ps. 100:4) and it releases great spiritual power (see 2 Chron. 5:13,14; 20:21-27; Acts 16:25,26). We often do not recognize that praise in itself can be a weapon of spiritual warfare to weaken the influence of the powers of evil and open the way for God to be glorified.

I remember Mel Tari telling of an incident in the Indonesian revival of 1965-1970 when he and his team were called to minister at a funeral in Timor. When they arrived, the body had been laid out for two days; it had not been embalmed and the smell of death was strong. But the people at the funeral believed God would raise the man from the dead and they asked Mel Tari to pray.

Instead of a prayer of petition, Tari chose a prayer of praise. He had the group form a circle around the corpse and sing a praise song to God. When nothing happened, they sang it again. When they sang it the sixth time, some toes began to move. The seventh time, the man opened his eyes. And the eighth time he got up and walked! Something obviously had happened in the heavenlies for that man to be a modern-day Lazarus and to overcome death. That time, the human means God used to manifest His glory was praise.

A POWER ENCOUNTER IN YAP

A friend of mine, Sam Sasser, served as an Assemblies of God missionary among the islands of the South Pacific. When he landed on Yap (a group of four small islands), he approached the chief and asked permission to preach the gospel to his people. The canny chief said that he would consider it, but first Sam had to pass some tests. The tests turned out to be athletic-type games with the men of Yap, and Sam did well.

The chief was obviously impressed, so Sam asked if he could now preach. "Not yet," said the chief. "There is one more game."

The men formed a large circle and began chanting and clapping, obviously invoking the power of the tribal principalities they had been serving. At the proper moment, 2 young girls entered the circle and started dancing in the center. Gradually, right before Sam's eyes, the girls began to levitate and soon were dancing in the air some 10 feet above the ground!

Smiling a sardonic smile, the chief said to Sam Sasser, "Can your God do that?"

Sam replied, "Sir, my God is not in the levitating business. But I'll tell you what He can do: He can make them come down!"

The power encounter was on. The powers of darkness had openly and visibly challenged the power of Jehovah God.

Sam Sasser positioned himself outside the circle, lifted his hands to heaven and began a steady stream of praise to the King of kings and Lord of lords. The girls plummeted to the ground, one injuring her ankle.

The astounded chief approached Sasser and said, "You may

now preach the gospel. We want to know more about your God."

Again, praise opened the way.

When Paul and Silas were in prison in Philippi the situation seemed hopeless. They were in stocks and in the inner prison for maximum security. What did they do? "At midnight Paul and Silas were praying and singing hymns to God" (Acts 16:25) and they were doing it loudly enough so the other prisoners heard them. An earthquake came, they were miraculously released and the jailer and his family were saved.

As in Indonesia and Yap, praise in Philippi released unusually dramatic supernatural power.

In summary, it is important to recognize that praise and worship are in themselves prayer. Cindy Jacobs says, "Worship is intercessory. It doesn't matter whether it is a current praise song or a song from the 1500s; it has power to break Satan's strongholds from hearts and minds."[4]

PRAISE ON CITY STREETS

Contemporary praise marches give us a vehicle to take our praise, using all its spiritual power, onto the city streets.

The March for Jesus is a new name, but not an entirely new concept. In the Old Testament, we see David leading a praise procession into Jerusalem (see 2 Sam. 6:12-17). In the New Testament, Jesus' Triumphal Entry was a joyous praise procession also into Jerusalem (see Matt. 21:1-9).

Graham Kendrick, in his definitive book on the subject, *Public Praise*, tells of how Aldhelm, the abbot of Malmesbury, took praise singing out into the streets of Wessex, England, in A.D. 675. John Huss went into the streets in Czechoslovakia in the fifteenth century. John Wesley, of course, preached in the open fields as well. But perhaps the strongest historic prototype comes from the Salvation Army in the nineteenth century, its brass bands becoming a common sight on the streets of England. Kendrick tells of one notable Salvation Army march in 1885, which "marched to the houses of Parliament with a petition two miles long, bearing 343,000 signatures demanding that the trade in child prostitution (which was rampant at the time) be stopped and the age of consent be raised from thirteen to sixteen years old. They succeeded."[5]

More recently, the Evangelism in Depth movement held 11 national, year-long crusades throughout Latin America in the 1960s, each having multiple praise marches. Luis Palau's evangelistic association often organizes marches, two of the largest being 700,000 in Guatemala City and 400,000 in Mexico City. Edgardo Silvoso's Harvest Evangelism organized a march drawing 18,000 in Buenos Aires, Argentina, in 1991. Kendrick tells of others in India under Bakht Singh and in China under Watchman Nee.[6]

UNDERSTANDING THE MARCH FOR JESUS

If we decide to take our praying into the community, and if one of the vehicles we choose for this is the March for Jesus,

---

A fundamental prerequisite for taking a city for God is substantial unity of the people of God, beginning with the pastors.

---

we should do it with excellence. If we put the bride of Christ on display and invite the general public to watch us worshiping our Lord and Master, it should be done with flair, dignity, exuberance, order, a cultural fit and with class. Fully understanding the what and why of the March for Jesus will help us accomplish just that.

The Purpose
The purpose of the Jesus March is to bring the whole Body of Christ to agreement in public praise to God.

It is my personal opinion that the March for Jesus has more potential for bringing about the unity of the Body of Christ across denominational lines and across racial lines than any other design available today.

As I have said many times, a fundamental prerequisite for taking a city for God is substantial unity of the people of God, beginning with the pastors. Concerts of prayer and particularly prayer summits have taken significant steps in that direction in many cities. The March for Jesus is not a substitute for either of those initiatives, but its simplicity does make it more immediately available to the entire Body of Christ, especially to families as a whole including children and youth. It is my personal opinion that the March for Jesus has more potential for bringing about the unity of the Body of Christ across denominational lines and across racial lines than any other design available today.

When analyzing what influence praise marches can make on a city, it is important to remind ourselves that in an important sense worship can be seen as an end in itself, not only a means to an end. Graham Kendrick says, "Worship is not so much a weapon as it is the very prize of the battle...the Father is seek-

ing worshippers upon whom to lavish His affection for eterni-
ty."[7] If we worship well and do nothing else, we please God.

We can expect praise marches to help bring unity to the
Body of Christ. We can expect strip clubs and illegal vice activities to be closed as they were after the 1985 Soho march in
London. But we need to go deeper than that. Graham
Kendrick's words are extremely important to anyone planning
to organize or participate in a March for Jesus: "What does all
this achieve? My answer is simple: the Lord receives worship.
Not only that, but humankind and angels watch Him receive
worship. Is that not an achievement of great significance in the
streets of a town or city where He is not normally honored?"[8]

The Principles

I recently heard Roger Forster, one of the originators of the
March for Jesus, list 10 fundamental principles of the March for
Jesus, each having theological undertones. They seem to cover
the whole spectrum, so I will list them here:

1. Obedience. We are obeying the desire of God that His
people make known to the nations His glory and majesty.

2. Visibility of the church. The church is too often seen
as irrelevant to the life of the community as a whole.

3. Unity of the Spirit. The church is seen as one people
despite differences in secondary doctrines, practices and styles
that otherwise keep Christian groups separate. John Dawson
says, "We are a nation that has brought reproach to the name of
the Lord through contention and division in the body of Christ.
There's no quicker way to overcome that than by the graphic
picture of thousands of believers marching together, physically,
side by side."[9]

4. Confession, repentance and reconciliation. Powerful
and moving public repentance is characteristically a part of the
public prayer meeting following a march.

5. Proclamation. This is done loudly and in unison.

6. Celebration. The festive atmosphere of a march produces great jubilation.

7. Prophetic symbolism. Public symbolic acts of many kinds are characteristic of Old Testament leaders such as Moses, Joshua and the prophets. The public praise march is a contemporary example.

8. Claiming ground. God's word to Joshua was, "Every place that the sole of your foot will tread upon I have given you" (Josh. 1:3). Forster says, "Why should the enemy have this territory? Why should he rule in our streets and control our economy? We put our feet down on a bit of territory and we say, 'Lord, this is Your ground....'"[10]

9. Boldness. Although the March for Jesus is not for the timid, neither does it admit only the lionhearted. Through it, average Christians can become bold for Christ.

10. Witness into the heavenly realm. Battles in the spiritual warfare needed to take a city for God are won through marches.

The Method

Logistical support for March for Jesus is in place. The London, England, office under Graham Kendrick and his colleagues manages the international affairs. They are strongly supported by the United States office in Austin, Texas, under Tom and Theresa Pelton. Other nations are developing their own national offices.

Each city that desires a March for Jesus should get in touch with one of these offices:

Outside of United States:
March for Jesus
P.O. Box 39
Sunbury-on-Thames
Middlesex, TW16 6PP
England

In United States:
March for Jesus
P.O. Box 3216
Austin, TX 78764
U.S.A.

These offices are prepared to supply the instructions necessary to organize a march from scratch.

The marches require as broad a base of citywide Christian leadership as possible. Careful planning is needed for the starting point and finishing point, having appropriate approval and permits from the municipality. A van equipped with an external sound system is required for every 200 to 300 marchers. Do's and don'ts of march etiquette are clearly spelled out. T-shirts and program songbooks are available.

Music for the Streets

During the march itself, all participants are singing, speaking and shouting the same things at the same time. The songs and liturgy for the English-speaking world are newly written each year by Graham Kendrick and published by Make Way Music.

The type of praise music suitable for the streets is different from the contemporary praise and worship music written for church gatherings. The praise and worship choruses that have become so popular today were largely written in connection with the charismatic renewal movement beginning in the 1960s. When these choruses first came out they were radical both in their musical style and their content, which appealed particularly to the baby boomer generation raised on rock music. The choruses were written as "love songs to Jesus" and dealt with the healing benefits Jesus could bring to hurting people who drew close to Him in worship. The thrust of this worship music was primarily to raise the level of spirituality of those who were already Christians. Very little of it was directed to the community outside the church or to the lost people out there.

Graham Kendrick surfaced a different kind of contemporary praise music, composed specifically with praise marches in mind. He says, "Many of the songs we sing indoors aren't suitable outdoors, both in style and content."[11]

"Shine, Jesus Shine" is the best-known song and is something of a theme song of Marches for Jesus. This new music, perhaps more than anything else, has the potential of turning the charismatic renewal, which has been mostly inward-looking, to a strong evangelistic force for God's Kingdom in these days. A song such as, "Let's go take this city, let's go fight in faith, For His Kingdom extends to the borders of this city" looks upward and outward, while "I love You, Lord, and I lift my voice to worship You" looks upward and inward.

There is some feeling today that the inward-looking, love-songs-to-Jesus type of worship is in danger of being exaggerated in some circles. One Christian leader, who stresses worship in his church, was recently affected when he sensed the Holy Spirit saying to him, "The world is dying without Jesus, and all the church is doing is singing songs!" Perhaps the Marches for Jesus and the new hymnology they are producing will help swing the pendulum back and allow God's people to get some walls down between the church and the community.

The Focus

It is obvious that the current growing popularity of praise marches could be hijacked by special interest groups to promote their own causes. This must be resisted strongly by Christians who are truly committed to taking their cities and nations for Christ. Graham Kendrick rightly says that such a hijacking could be a "kiss of death" for the March for Jesus. He draws on his experience and carefully outlines nine things that the March for Jesus is *not*:

1. Marches are not protests.
2. Marches are not built around issues, but around a Person.
3. Marches are not critical or confrontational.
4. Marches are not a publicity stunt.
5. Marches are not an evangelistic campaign.

6. Marches are not presented as a method of spiritual warfare.
7. Marches are not a ritual.
8. Marches are not triumphalism.
9. Marches are not personality-centered.[12]

As has been said, the focus of the march must be first and foremost a public declaration by Christians of all stripes that Jesus Christ is exalted and that He is the rightful King of kings and Lord of lords over the city.

The Outcome

A March for Jesus produces a change in the spiritual atmosphere of the city.

This is such a bold statement that it requires immediate qualification. For one thing, because we are dealing here with the effect of a visible march on the invisible world, we have removed ourselves from the possibility of totally objective measurements. But such is the case with all prayer, as I pointed out earlier in the book. Only our faith in God and obedience to His Word can assure us that His promises concerning answered prayer are being kept. When we do see tangible changes in the spread of righteousness and justice in our community and numbers of unsaved people coming to Christ, our confidence rises.

The second qualification has to do with degree. Change has taken place in the invisible world, but how much? A trap that many naive Christian leaders can fall into is to suspect that by having 1, 2 or 10 Marches for Jesus the territorial spirits over a city will be torn down, bound and dispatched. This kind of nonsense is what prompts Graham Kendrick to say, "I don't subscribe to the view that the aim of a praise march is to exorcise a town or an institution from demonic influence. A march is not a cure-all for all the ills in a town, nor is it a substitute for everyday witness and social action."[13] For this reason he also says, as we have just seen, "Marches are not presented as a method of spiritual warfare."

By this we do not mean that spiritual warfare is not one of the outcomes of a March for Jesus. Kendrick says, "Coming together in a spirit of unity is itself a powerful act of spiritual warfare. It declares to the powers of darkness that they are disarmed and doomed because in Christ we are reconciled and brought together in love at the foot of the cross."[14]

Praise marches should not be seen as settings for the direct types of confrontation with principalities, powers and strongholds that some prayer journeys I will describe later would do. There is a time and place for them as well, but the March for Jesus is neither the time nor the place.

Marches for Jesus are a kind of demonstration to the powers in heavenly places in which the whole family can participate. Other forms of spiritual warfare are definitely adults only.

In any case, when we participate in a March for Jesus, we help fulfill God's desire that "the manifold wisdom of God might be made known by the church to the principalities and powers in the heavenly places" (Eph. 3:10).

■ REFLECTION QUESTIONS ■

1. Have you personally participated in a March for Jesus? If so, describe your feelings. If not, does this sound like something that could be implemented in your city?
2. If the March for Jesus in Nürnberg did have some influence in changing the attitude of German Christians, what theological explanation could you give? What could have happened in the invisible world?
3. Talk about the concept that praise is a form of prayer. Can you give other examples of the tangible power of praise?

4. What does Graham Kendrick mean when he says, "Worship is not so much a weapon as it is the very prize of the battle"?
5. Review and discuss the list of nine things that a March for Jesus is *not*. At the same time, can you find a *positive* sense for each of the items?

Notes

1. Graham Kendrick, Gerald Coates, Roger Forster and Lynn Green with Catherine Butcher, *March for Jesus* (Eastbourne, England: Kingsway Publications, 1992), p. 26.
2. George Jones, "Graham Kendrick: Taking Worship Into the Streets," *Ministries Today*, November-December 1991, p. 48.
3. Randy Robison and John Archer, "Praise Him in the Streets," *Charisma and Christian Life*, May 1992, p. 22.
4. Cindy Jacobs, *Possessing the Gates of the Enemy* (Grand Rapids, MI: Chosen Books, 1991), p. 181.
5. Graham Kendrick, *Public Praise* (Altamonte Springs, FL: Creation House, 1992), p. 53.
6. Ibid., pp. 54-58.
7. Ibid., p. 60.
8. Ibid., p. 19.
9. Robison and Archer, "Praise Him in the Streets," p. 26.
10. Kendrick, et. al., *March for Jesus*, pp. 149,150.
11. Ibid., pp. 24,25.
12. Kendrick, *Public Praise*, pp. 20-22.
13. Jones, "Graham Kendrick," p. 51.
14. Kendrick, *Public Praise*, p. 103.

Prayerwalks

P RAISE MARCHES FOCUS PRIMARILY ON THE CITY. PRAYER-
walks focus primarily on neighborhoods. Both help
to get the walls down between the church and the
community.

MOVING INTO THE STREETS

Andrés Miranda is the pastor of a small Church of God
in Montevideo, Uruguay, and also the editor of the
Uruguayan national Christian newspaper, *El Puente.*

He was called to be the pastor of a church that was
25 years old and stagnant. The church had 25 members
when he accepted the call.

Miranda worked hard during the first year and the
church grew to 80. Although he saw some rapid
growth, he also knew deep down that the people were
not getting fed with the solid Bible teaching they need-

ed. In retrospect, he admitted that he was building the church too much on his own personal ambitions rather than on sound church growth principles. He began praying about it, searching his heart and keeping himself open to hear from God.

God did speak to Andrés Miranda. He told him that he should take his people outside of the walls of the church to pray in their community. He sensed that they should not do this as an ongoing part of their church life, but they were to do it at least one time. They had never done it before.

He decided to move into the streets on a Sunday as part of their regular service. They began in the church auditorium and divided into four groups for what we now call prayerwalks. Each group went to one of the four corners of the nearby intersection and prayed fervently for their city and their neighborhood. On one of the corners stood the local temple of Macumba spiritism, which had come into Uruguay from neighboring Brazil years previously. They did not single out the temple for targeted, spiritual warfare, but they prayed for God's power and His glory to come to their neighborhood.

After they prayed for a time, each group began to walk down one of the four streets for one block, praying for the people and the families and the businesses as they walked. Then they regrouped and went on with life as usual.

A Backlash and a Cleansing
Two unusual things happened.

First, for no apparent reason the Macumba temple, which had been functioning on the corner for years, closed down. Because the Christians were not in contact with the spiritists, they never did discover exactly why it closed. They later found that the people who led it had opened a new temple almost 100 miles away. Whatever, the neighborhood they prayed for was no longer a local Macumba center.

Second, a spiritual backlash struck the church. Evil spirits began manifesting in the congregation from time to time. Pastor Miranda rose to the occasion, rebuked them and cast them out, but some must have remained because the church entered a period of dissension and confusion. Church members began to leave; almost all of the 80 members eventually decided to go elsewhere.

At first Miranda was discouraged and downhearted. But as the exodus continued it was becoming clearer and clearer to him that the church had been harboring serious spiritual problems of which he had not been aware. Some of these had been building up for 25 years, and they finally were exposed and dealt with openly. The congregation was reduced to practically nothing, but by then Miranda realized he was witnessing a thorough cleansing, more needed in his church than he had imagined.

Then the blessing began to come. A few months later, the last I have heard, the congregation had grown back to 50, but now 80 percent of the members are new converts, something that had never been true before. And even more encouraging, many of the new converts are from the very block where the church is located. They have provided a medical clinic for the people in the neighborhood, a day-care center and are giving free breakfasts to poor children. What the enemy meant for evil, God turned into good. They now believe firmly that the entire block will be Christian before very long.

And the change? It came from a simple prayerwalk after the Church of God decided to get the wall down between the church and the community.

PRINCIPLES OF PRAYERWALKING

Steve Hawthorne, who, along with Graham Kendrick, is in the process of authoring the definitive book on the subject, defines prayerwalking (they prefer it as one word) as *praying on site with insight.* "This is intercessory prayer," Hawthorne says, "praying in the very place in which you expect your prayers to be answered."[1]

The idea of praying *on site* brings the pray-ers into the community. It helps implement a theme verse for the 1990s: "Every place that the sole of your foot will tread upon, I have given you" (Josh. 1:3). The idea of walking brings us into the closest contact with those in the community for whom we are praying. The walking, of course, does not have to be perpetual motion. Once we walk into our community we can stand, sit or lie down on the grass as we pray. Hawthorne says, "It's not just your feet—with your feet the rest of your person is there: body, soul, mind, and spirit. Where you choose to put your body, your spirit can also function full force."[2]

Praying with *insight* brings to our attention one of the most promising of the newer innovations of the prayer movement: spiritual mapping. The third book in this *Prayer Warrior* series, *Breaking Strongholds in Your City*, is on that very subject. We are learning that targeted prayers can be more effective than vague, scattered prayers when we are interceding for a city or a neighborhood.

Insight can come from researching the historical and physical aspects of a city or neighborhood, and also from simple observation of what turns up as you are walking through. Add to this spiritual discernment and hearing directly from God about what needs prayer, and prayerwalkers can begin to pray with a considerable degree of accuracy.

Spiritual mapping per se is not called for particularly as a preparation for a March for Jesus except to determine with intelligence the parade route, particularly the starting and finishing points. But because a praise march is not usually designed for overt, intentional spiritual warfare, mapping is a lower priority. It becomes useful for more advanced prayerwalking, although spiritual mapping by no means should be considered a prerequisite for beginning prayerwalks. Later in this chapter I will explain how John Huffman has developed a simplified form of mapping specifically for prayerwalks.

When we move on to prayer expeditions and prayer journeys, spiritual mapping becomes a vital part of the process and I will discuss it more in chapters 9 and 10.

WHO FIRST PRAYERWALKED?

Back in the days when walking was the major form of transportation from one location to another, many Christians must have prayed as they went from one town to another. Graham Kendrick and John Houghton found a reference to prayerwalking written by Hermas in *The Shepherd* in A.D. 180: "While then I am walking alone, I entreat the Lord that He will accomplish the revelations and visions which He showed me through

---

A nice thing about prayerwalking is that anyone can do it. They can be plain, everyday Christians who love the Lord and who believe that God is calling His people these days not only to pray for their community, but to pray *in* their community.

His holy Church, that He may strengthen me and may give repentance to His servants which have stumbled, that His great and glorious name may be glorified."[3]

Further indications that serious prayerwalking was done by

such notables as Saint Patrick, John Wycliffe, George Fox and others can also be found.

Steve Hawthorne's extensive research on the modern prayerwalking movement has uncovered no one person or one event that initiated it. He found hundreds of examples of prayerwalking that had no relationship to each other at all. Very little coordination of prayerwalking has been done on national or local levels. Nevertheless, Hawthorne says, "I have yet to find a bona fide sustained prayerwalking effort before about the mid-1970s."[4] Since that time, however, prayerwalking activities have mushroomed in many parts of the world.

ENTRY-LEVEL SPIRITUAL WARFARE

A nice thing about prayerwalking is that, like the March for Jesus, anyone can do it. Prayerwalkers do not have to be Bible school graduates, ordained ministers, over 18, gifted intercessors, eloquent speakers, spiritual giants or particularly courageous. They can be plain, everyday Christians who love the Lord and who believe that God is calling His people these days not only to pray *for* their community, but to pray *in* their community. And they need to be committed enough to this ministry to block out regular time on their schedules for prayerwalking.

Unlike Marches for Jesus, prayerwalks do not have to be highly organized and coordinated. No permits are needed from city hall. Special training is not required, although with good training this ministry can move to a more advanced stage and become more effective.

Spiritually speaking, prayerwalking is relatively safe. Although it is a form of overt spiritual warfare, the dangers are not nearly as great as other spiritual engagements, especially if the commonsense guidelines in this chapter are followed. Steve Hawthorne says, "I haven't had reports of casualties in prayerwalking, if it's wisely done. To the extent that prayerwalking your city is spiritual warfare, it seems to be a very basic warfare operation, not Purple-Heart kind of stuff."[5]

VARIETIES OF PRAYERWALKS

Having hundreds of prayerwalks conducted daily in many parts of our nation and the world, it is obvious that many varieties of prayerwalks will have emerged. Because one of our responsibilities in the United Prayer Track of the A.D. 2000 Movement is to coordinate worldwide prayer activities to the degree possible, we have worked hard to attempt to define certain terms. The four technical terms we have now agreed upon are: (1) praise marches; (2) prayerwalks; (3) prayer expeditions; and (4) prayer journeys. To the extent that we can have consensus on the meaning of these terms, communication within the Body of Christ will be facilitated.

In the past, "prayerwalking" has been used by some as a catchall term. Almost any prayer ministry in the community has been called "prayerwalking" by some. This state of affairs is mutually recognized by top-level prayer leaders and we are now trying not to use the term "prayerwalking" to describe, for example, what we agree would be better called a "prayer expedition" or a "prayer journey," although undoubtedly the terms will overlap and be used interchangeably by some.

The major kind of prayerwalking I will detail in this chapter is praying for neighborhoods, particularly the neighborhood in which one lives. By this, however, I do not mean to imply that other ways of doing prayerwalking are not legitimate. There is not, nor should there ever be, some officially accredited way of prayerwalking. God is a God of great variety, and He delights to lead His children in different ways. The major rule is to follow whatever God's Spirit is saying.

Here are some examples of the way prayerwalking is being done today:

- Jorge Plourde is the National Prayer Director for the Dominican Republic Confederation of Evangelicals. As part of their interdenominational prayer activity, they pray for the public parks of the capital city of Santo Domingo. On the third Saturday of each month, teams of intercessors go to each one of the parks to pray for three hours, from 2:00 P.M. to 5:00 P.M. They conclude each session by doing warfare prayer as they walk around the perimeters of each park.
- The capital city of Santo Domingo is also covered through street-corner praying. A team of 400 intercessors meet together periodically and they divide into 40 groups of 10 each. They pray for 1 hour on the 4 corners of 10 consecutive intersections up and down a particular street. Then at the end of the hour they all walk 1 block in the same direction and cover the next 10 intersections for another hour.
- Pastor Steven Bunkoff of the Savannah, New York, Congregational Church decided to canvass every home in their town. But they did not distribute literature or ring doorbells. All they did was to pray for each house and those inside. A large map in the sanctuary depicted their progress, and the project took 25 weeks. The pastor reports, "People began visiting our church, and there was no 'natural' explanation—other than that we prayed. One Sunday four families from one street came after one week of praying for them."
- Three college students daily prayerwalk their dormitories and pray for their fellow students.
- Parents prayerwalk around their children's schools.
- A church decides to move the whole Sunday School

out of the church facility one Sunday morning and lead the people in prayerwalking the streets surrounding the church.
- A Christian nurse uses coffee breaks to walk the corridors of the hospital, praying for the patients and the staff.

NEIGHBORHOOD PRAYERWALKS

One major reason for making neighborhoods a primary focus for prayerwalking is the biblical concept of territoriality. Those who actually reside in an area presumably can exercise a greater spiritual authority than can outsiders. This applies to nations, cities, industries, people groups and other human networks as well as to neighborhoods.

Doris and I have ministered in international strategic-level spiritual warfare a good deal with Cindy Jacobs of Generals of Intercession. She is in considerable demand as a consultant for spiritual-warfare initiatives in many cities and countries. Wherever she goes, she is careful to explain to local leaders the relationship of territoriality to authority. She does not allow them to imagine that she, as an outsider, has come to do the strategic-level intercession the situation may call for.

We recently were with Cindy in Brasilia, Brazil, where she led a group of 105 seasoned Brazilian intercessors in on-site prayer for the nation. Although Cindy did a good bit of coaching, she did none of the praying because she had no territorial authority. The Brazilians did the praying.

However, outsiders can move into a territory not their own to pray. As we will see in the following chapters, prayer expeditions and prayer journeys are mostly done by outsiders. In such cases, however, clear guidance from God is advised. In contrast, prayerwalking one's own neighborhood can emerge from resolution, not necessarily revelation. The same applies to the members of a church prayerwalking the church's neighborhood whether they live there or not.

BIBLICAL TERRITORIALITY

The idea of territorial authority begins with Adam and Eve in the garden of Eden. The garden God gave them to tend was obviously within certain geographical boundaries. This becomes clear after the Fall when God sent Adam "out of the garden of Eden to till the ground from which he was taken" and positioned cherubim to guard it so Adam could not get back in (see Gen. 3:23,24).

The apostle Paul hinted that his authority had territorial limits when he wrote to the Corinthians that he would confine his boasting to the "field God has assigned to us" (2 Cor. 10:13, *NIV*). Later, he wrote, "We do not want to boast about work already done in another man's territory" (2 Cor. 10:16, *NIV*).

God promised His people that if they would humble themselves, pray, seek His face and turn from their wicked ways, He would hear them, forgive their sin and *"heal their land"* (2 Chron. 7:14, emphasis mine). He did not say He would heal the land of the Egyptians or the Chinese or the Aztecs, but rather their portion of geography. This was the land over which God's people had inherent authority.

When God's people were sent into exile in Babylonia, the fact that they resided there gave them a measure of authority. "And seek the peace of the city where I have caused you to be carried away captive, and pray to the Lord for it" (Jer. 29:7). This helps us to understand that we not only have authority in neighborhoods where we may own property, but also where we rent an apartment or a room or teach in a school or pastor a church or where some other legal means establishes territoriality.

Unpacking Beckett's Bags

My friend Bob Beckett, a leader in the spiritual-mapping field, confesses that he was frustrated and disappointed with the way his ministry was going in his church and in his community until the Lord strongly impressed on him and his wife, Susan, the need for a pastor to make a territorial commitment for ministry.

Beckett said that if his city were ever to experience significant deliverance from the principalities of darkness over it, "Someone like me needed to begin by unpacking their bags and setting aside their dreams of a more exciting ministry in the future. Pastors, lay leaders and whole churches must join, taking long-term territorial responsibility for the land they are living in!"[6]

When Bob and Susan announced they were staying in their city of Hemet, California, and had purchased cemetery plots to help seal the territorial commitment, the community started changing and their church started growing.

As American Christians living in a mobile society, it may be that we have not taken biblical territoriality as seriously as we might. The more we understand this, the more powerful can be our ministry to our immediate neighborhoods. I believe that in these days God wishes to raise up a veritable army of plain Christians who live in plain neighborhoods to get serious about their territory. The major cost for ministering to a neighborhood through prayerwalking is time. Believers who are willing to give the time will thereby put themselves on the cutting edge of one of the exciting things God is doing in the 1990s.

I see two general ways of prayerwalking in neighborhoods. One is spontaneous and the other is synchronized. Let's look at them one at a time.

SPONTANEOUS PRAYERWALKING

A church, a family, a home-cell group or any circle of Christians can receive a burden for praying for their neighborhood on their own. Whether others in the city or in the neighborhood are also doing it makes little difference for this spontaneous type of prayerwalk.

Brian Gregory, an Anglican minister in Platt Bridge, Wigan, England, sensed that God wanted his people to prayerwalk the 90 streets within the border of his parish. He alphabetized the 90 streets and asked his congregation to pray for 2 of the streets each week in alphabetical order. They now also pray for the people on those 2 designated streets in the Sunday morning service. On Monday, teams go to every home on the 2 streets and distribute a leaflet showing a picture of Jesus and a notice that they are being prayed for that week. Each Wednesday morning at 8:00 A.M. a prayerwalking team walks the 2 streets in intercession for the people there.

Later, they distribute another leaflet inviting the people to submit prayer requests or to invite the team into their homes for prayer. After doing this for four years, Gregory reports, "Prayerwalking has become as much a characteristic of community life as the beat policeman, and has been featured in the local press." And the outcome? "The crime rate has dropped, the spiritual atmosphere improved and slum housing has been replaced....Relationships have improved between ministers and local churches. And more people are joining the church."[7]

Cheese, Honey and Prayer

A Puerto Rican student of mine planted a Hispanic church in East Los Angeles while he was doing graduate studies. One day he told me that the government was distributing free cheese and honey to the residents of the area and that his church had been selected as a distribution center. He needed only to provide the volunteer personnel. As a requirement to receive the food, each resident had to fill out a form including their name and address and a complete list of all those who lived in their house. My student said, "What shall I do with all those names?"

I asked him how traditional door-to-door witnessing had worked, and he said very poorly. It was the answer I expected, so I said, "Why don't we try something different? Why don't we try prayer?"

I suggested that he ask all who were willing to participate in this outreach to gather one hour early for the weekly Wednesday night prayer meeting and come at 6:30. They would break up into teams of three and be given a certain number of the forms that had been filled out. Each team would visit a few of those families, telling them that they were from the church that gave them the honey and cheese, and in a short time they were going to gather for prayer, asking them for things they would like the church to pray about. Each team would carry a clipboard to note the prayer requests. The next week they would visit again, see if the prayer had been answered and take more requests.

They were to maintain the mentality that this was not an evangelistic visit. They were not to invite the families to come to church. They were simply to offer prayer.

It worked so well that the pastor was elated. The church gained a very positive image in the community and in six months it had grown so much they had to look for a new facility!

Getting Started

Possibilities are endless. Some may be saying by now, "This is something I would like to try. How can I get started?" Here are some suggestions:

- Tell your pastor you feel you should begin to pray in your neighborhood and would he or she bless you and pray for you before you begin. Few pastors would turn down such a request. This is more important than some might think, because when your pastor prays for you, you receive imputed spiritual authority you would not otherwise have. It can be a valuable source of spiritual protection against possible attacks of the enemy.

- Form a team. Visit other Christians in your neighborhood to see if God may be calling any of them to prayerwalk with you. Aim for a minimum of three and a maximum of six. Plan *A* should be to recruit believers from other churches than your own. The more the whole Body of Christ is represented, the better. Plan *B* is a team made up of those from your own church.

- Set a schedule, starting with 1 prayerwalk a week. Spend 15 minutes together in preparation, then move into the neighborhood for 30 to 45 minutes. Gather in a group on 1 intersection and pray 1 at a time for the 4 blocks that meet at the intersection. Pray with your eyes open for what you see with your eyes and also for what God may show you in your spirit. When you finish, choose one of the 4 streets and walk slowly up 1 side of the block and back the other, praying as you walk.

The next week you may start at a different intersection, but do not spread yourselves too thin. As the weeks go by, your prayer team should be a familiar neighborhood sight and some may begin to ask what you are doing. Tell them, and offer to pray specifically for them or their family right on the spot. If you are invited to pray inside their home, make an appointment and return at another time.

Follow these instructions for a starter, then as you gain experience make any number of variations regarding frequency, time and methodology that you feel God is indicating. Let your imagination take over.

Spiritual Warfare

Do not forget that although neighborhood prayerwalking is not especially dangerous, it is a form of spiritual warfare. Be sure

---

Prayerwalking,...is no substitute for ongoing evangelism and social ministry. But it can greatly help clear the way spiritually for the other things to happen.

---

you are in proper spiritual condition week by week to do it. Cindy Jacobs has some excellent advice: "Before you begin your prayerwalk, it is important to dress yourself spiritually for the battle just as you would dress appropriately for other occasions. Stop and pray before you head out the door and clothe yourself with the armor of God. Pray for protection for yourself, your home and your family according to Psalm 91."[8]

John Dawson, who lives in a depressed part of Los Angeles, tells of how he took his staff for a prayerwalk through his neighborhood. "We stood in front of every house," he says, "rebuked Satan's work in Jesus' name and prayed for a revelation of Jesus in the life of each family." He says there is still a long way to go, but "social, economic and spiritual transformation is evident."[9]

One prayerwalk was not a quick fix for the neighborhood. The Dawsons have made a territorial commitment to their neighborhood and they are constantly praying for and ministering to their neighbors. Prayerwalking, like praise marches, is no substitute for ongoing evangelism and social ministry. But it can greatly help clear the way spiritually for the other things to happen.

SYNCHRONIZED PRAYERWALKING

Most prayerwalking to date has been spontaneous. Ministry and results have been good. But suppose we went beyond doing it here and there. Suppose that once a week every single block of every single street in your city were covered by a prayerwalk. Could you believe that within a year it would be a different city? I believe it would, but it would take more effort, more leadership and more coordination.

My friend John Huffman has pioneered the kind of citywide neighborhood prayerwalking that might give us the clues about how to do it in our own city. His initial field experiments, called "Christ for the City," were done in Medellín, Colombia.

Because this is a citywide effort, the pastors and Christian leaders of the city should be unified to the degree possible in their support for this prayer effort. They need to encourage their church members to participate in their neighborhood's prayer initiative. Some who know the city well should draw the boundaries of manageable neighborhoods. Neighborhood coordinators should then be recruited in as many of the neighborhoods as possible.

Prayer for Evangelism

Although all synchronized neighborhood prayerwalking does not have to be this way, John Huffman's plan is explicitly evangelistic. But prayer is not to be seen as just another evangelistic method. The Christian community already has many excellent evangelistic methods in place and has believers trained in how to apply them. Huffman says, "Our basic idea is to apply the biblical principles of spiritual warfare through prayer *before* one begins to evangelize."[10] Once the spiritual warfare is done well, we will "bind or incapacitate the prince of this world long enough for many to adequately hear the Gospel,"[11] and then we can apply most any evangelistic methodology to reap the harvest God desires to give us.

The general idea is to mobilize as massive an amount of

intercessory prayer for the neighborhood as possible for 14 days preceding an evangelistic event. The more targeted the prayer the better, so each neighborhood is mapped block by block. A single sheet of paper is used for identifying each square block. Houses, stores, parks, schools, vacant lots, apartment buildings and whatever are then located on the 4 sides of the block. For each house, the house number is given, the name of the family, the color of the house and other identifying features. When the maps are ready, copies are given to members of the on-site prayer teams, and also sent to any number of intercessors in other parts of the city or nation, as well as to other nations who have agreed to join in prayer for those 2 weeks.

A suggested prayer program for the 2 weeks has been outlined by Huffman, but any variations the Lord indicates are welcome. The schedule includes, among other things, preparation of the intercessors, prayers of blessing, warfare praying, fasting and prayer for special groups. On site, teams prayerwalk the neighborhood for at least 2 of the 14 days, stopping for visits in places previously indicated through words the Lord has given to intercessors both nearby and far away.

Uncovering a Curse

In a two-week prayer effort in Medellín, a prayer group from a Baptist General Conference church in North Dakota had agreed to pray. Like many traditional evangelicals, they were not particularly experienced in hearing from God in two-way prayer, but they did hear. God told them clearly that some evil force needed to be dealt with in a certain vacant lot on one of the maps. The word was so strong that they faxed the information to Colombia.

The neighborhood team in Colombia visited the vacant lot and asked God to show them what was wrong. He showed them that witches had buried five occult objects there to curse the Christ for the City initiative. They dug up the objects, destroyed them, broke the curse and prayed God's blessing on the neighborhood and on those who buried the objects. Many people were saved.

The Results

To the degree possible, John Huffman keeps records of what happens in Christ for the City. During 4 years of praying for neighborhoods in Medellín, which incidentally is the center of the Colombian drug Mafia, the number of evangelical churches increased from 93 to 140 and the number of believers increased 133 percent, from 4,434 to 10,350.

While Christ for the City was in operation, the Every Home for Christ team was also at work distributing Christian literature systematically to every home in the city. The team enrolled as many as possible in a Bible study course and invited those who finished the course to receive Christ, then sign a card affirming that they had done so. The two activities were mutually supportive but not explicitly coordinated with each other.

An amazing fact emerged. When Every Home for Christ personnel went to a neighborhood that did not yet have a team that had prayerwalked the neighborhood, only 10 percent of those who accepted the first Bible study finished the series and signed the card. But in the neighborhoods that had been covered by prayer, the 10 percent went up to 55 percent!

Little doubt remains that prayerwalking can change the spiritual atmosphere of a neighborhood and allow the gospel of the glory of Christ to shine brightly.

■ REFLECTION QUESTIONS ■

1. After prayerwalking, the church in Uruguay experienced a drastic loss of members. Would you think this was the work of Satan or the Holy Spirit? Why?

2. One of the most radical points of this chapter is the concept of the relationship of territoriality to spiritual authority. Discuss your opinion of this, especially referring to Bob and Susan Beckett's decision to stay in Hemet, California.
3. What do you think of the way the Anglicans in England prayerwalked 90 streets? Does this sound like something people in your church would be interested in?
4. Has your pastor ever mentioned prayerwalking to the congregation? If not, do you think he or she would be open to reading this chapter and consider encouraging this ministry in the community?
5. Prayer is not evangelism. But talk about the role that prayer did have in the evangelization of Medellín, Columbia, under Christ for the City.

Notes
1. Steve Hawthorne, "Prayerwalking," *Body Life*, December 1992, p. 1.
2. Ibid., p. 6.
3. Graham Kendrick and John Houghton, *Prayerwalking* (Eastbourne, England: Kingsway Publications, 1990), p. 24.
4. Hawthorne, "Prayerwalking," p. 1.
5. Ibid., p. 6.
6. Bob Beckett, "Steps Toward Community Deliverance," *Breaking Strongholds in Your City*, C. Peter Wagner, ed. (Ventura, CA: Regal Books, 1993), p. 163.
7. Kendrick and Houghton, *Prayerwalking*, p. 35.
8. Cindy Jacobs, *Possessing the Gates of the Enemy* (Grand Rapids, MI: Chosen Books, 1991), p. 219.
9. John Dawson, *Taking Our Cities for God* (Lake Mary, FL: Creation House, 1989), pp. 28,29.
10. John C. Huffman, *Christ for the City Manual of Participatory Prayer* (Christ for the City, P.O. Box 52-7900, Miami, FL 33152-7900, 1992), p. 3
11. Ibid., p. 5.

Prayer Expeditions

N E

IN 1991, SWITZERLAND CELEBRATED THE 700TH ANNIVERsary of its nationhood.

In 1990, a Swiss deaconess who had a strong ministry of intercession heard the call of God to lead a prayer expedition. She was to pray around the national boundaries of Switzerland!

PRAYING THE BORDERS OF SWITZERLAND

The Swiss deaconess recruited 2 prayer partners to join her, forming a nucleus of 3. They started in Lausanne and set their course to walk the periphery of each of the 12 Swiss provinces that outline the borders of the nation. She held seminars on intercession in the capital cities of each of the provinces, inviting people from the local churches to join them in the expedition. On some days, only the nucleus of 3 was walking, but on other days up to 50 participated. The average was 8 a day.

The expedition took 11 weeks. Each morning the group gathered at 9:00 A.M. for devotions and prayer. Depending on the terrain, they would ordinarily cover 9 to 12 miles a day. They walked silently for the first half hour, tuning in spiritually to the directions God would give them for their prayers that day. As they continued walking, they shared with each other what they felt they had been hearing from God. They then prayed aloud as they walked for the next 1 to 2 hours. Two of the prayer themes that came up the most frequently were: (1) to pray that God would raise up a new generation of Christian leaders in Switzerland who would not be shackled by the traditions built up over 700 years; and (2) that children would somehow be powerfully used in God's Kingdom in Switzerland. They, of course, prayed for many other things as well.

FOCUSING ON REGIONS

Praise marches focus primarily on cities. Prayerwalks focus primarily on neighborhoods. Prayer expeditions (which have also been called "prayerwalks" in the past)[1], such as the one in Switzerland, focus primarily on regions. The deaconess's team was praying outside the walls of their church, this time for their entire nation.

Couldn't they have gathered in a comfortable church sanctuary and prayed for their nation instead of climbing up and down all those Alps? Of course, and God will continue to lead many of His people to continue doing just that. But in these days it seems that He is also calling some of His people to engage in a bolder, more public kind of prayer. A word from God that I have mentioned frequently is: "Every place that the sole of your foot will tread upon, I have given you" (Josh. 1:3). Graham Kendrick and John Houghton say that the great merit of a prayer expedition "is the sheer breadth of praying which it generates, and often national and international issues become clear in a way that is missed on the shorter walks."[2]

Prayer expeditions, like prayerwalking, have no one who could be regarded as a founder. The Holy Spirit has been speaking to many Christian leaders in diverse and unconnected ministries to take their prayers out to the general public. Predictably, among those who have pioneered prayer expeditions is the same group of innovators in London that also influenced praise marches and prayerwalking.

The vision came in part when God spoke to them through Isaiah 35:8: "A highway shall be there, and a road, and it shall be called the Highway of Holiness," and later that the ransomed of the Lord shall come on this highway "with singing, with everlasting joy on their heads" (Isa. 35:10). The first prayer expedition was conducted simultaneously from John O'Groats, Scotland, to London, England, meeting up with the other one from Land's End in the south of England to London.[3]

God also spoke to them through the geographical references in Isaiah 43:5,6: "I will bring your descendants from the east, and gather you from the west; I will say to the north, 'Give them up!' and to the south, 'Do not keep them back!'"

THE TRAIL OF THE WORLD'S UNWORTHY

Gwen Shaw, founder of End-Time Handmaidens and a charter member of the Spiritual Warfare Network, sensed recently that God was sending her, along with her husband, Jim, on a prayer expedition following the trails of persecuted believers "of whom the world was not worthy" as the writer of Hebrews might characterize them (see Heb. 11:38). Her focus was on her ancestral Europe, and God deeply impressed her with the atrocities perpetrated upon such groups as the Cathars, the Huguenots, the Lutherans, the Anabaptists, the Mennonites, the

Hutterites, the Moravians and others. She felt that some of the sins committed against these groups by Christians were maintaining a negative effect on the spiritual atmosphere of Europe today.

In the summer of 1992, the Shaws were able to visit and pray over sites that the Cathars, the Huguenots and the Moravians had occupied. The Cathars of southern France, who held some doctrines that the traditional church considered unacceptable, were totally wiped out in the 1200s. As many as 140 at once, regardless of age, were burned to death on huge flaming pyres.

Gwen Shaw reports: "We visited almost all of these sites, and prayed, asking God to remove the curse of shedding innocent blood from southern France, beseeching God to extend His mercy and send a great and merciful revival upon the descendants of those who had done these evil deeds."[4]

They spent several hours in prayer in the secret desert headquarters where persecuted Huguenots had fled for their lives. They did the same in the former Moravian refuge in Eastern Germany where the Moravians retreated after being driven from their homelands in southern Czechoslovakia.

Sister Gwen writes, "Yes, we followed the 'trail of tears,' tears that our fathers and mothers of the faith marked out for us by their courage, dedication and love for God—people of 'whom the world was not worthy.'"[5]

LONDON TO BERLIN

The most extensive and best-organized prayer expedition I am aware of at this writing was organized in 1992 by the London team of Roger Forster, Gerald Coates, Lynn Green and Graham Kendrick. It covered an 800-mile route from London to Berlin and intercessors from 6 nations participated. The team varied in size, up to 30 at different points of the route. Ten of the team walked the whole route.[6] As time passes, I believe God will bring forth many such expeditions, some undoubtedly more sophisticated, as we collectively gain experience.

But, at the moment, the London to Berlin expedition can be regarded as a prototype. By this I would not advocate that every prayer expedition be carried out in the same way, but issues raised and lessons learned in the London to Berlin expedition will help us greatly to understand the concept.

WHERE SHOULD AN EXPEDITION BE LAUNCHED?

Prayer expeditions are somewhat more advanced in their scope and complexity than praise marches or prayerwalks. Those who plan them should have some experience in high-level intercession. They should know what it is to "pray in the Spirit" as Ephesians 6:18 says. Whether to have an expedition at all, where to have it and when to have it are such important questions that a clear mandate should come from God. Prayer expeditions could easily become trivialized or routinized and we can believe that Satan would like to see this happen. His domain is seriously threatened by Christians moving out in powerful intercession through a region.

God gave the vision for a London to Berlin expedition as the plans for the first "European Day" March for Jesus developed for May 23, 1992. Although marches were to be held on that day in 40 European cities, it seemed right to prepare the way for them by having a 31-day prayer expedition throughout the region. The March for Jesus organizers in Berlin were finding unusual response to the concept of Christians celebrating a unified Germany, particularly if they could march and praise God under the Brandenburg Gate, which had symbolized the division.

Berlin, therefore, seemed to be the right city toward which

the expedition should move. London was the home base of the organizers, and adequate office facilities were already in place to provide the needed logistical support. Certainly a spiritual link between the most prominent cities of the United Kingdom and Germany would also have a Pan-European political significance just at the time the European Common Market was opening. The consensus emerged that London to Berlin was the way God was leading.

Once this expedition was announced, prayer leaders in other parts of Europe felt that they should also be a part. Four ancillary expeditions were then organized, each one as a tributary to the London-Berlin stream:

- A team was to walk through Ireland from Port Stewart to Dublin and join the expedition in Dover, England.
- A team was to walk from Paris and join the expedition in Calais, France.
- A team was to walk from Amsterdam and join the expedition in Maastricht, Netherlands.
- A team was to walk from Tübingen and join the expedition in Braunschweig, Germany.

CASTING A NET OF PRAYER

In August 1992, Women's Aglow Fellowship sensed that God was leading them to "cast a net of prayer" over the United States. Jane Hansen, Bobbye Byerly, Doris Eaker and other Aglow leaders challenged area boards in every state to participate, and they did. Although there was room for much local creativity, two general suggestions were made.

The first was that each state should be covered in prayer: east to west, north to south. Some walked, some drove, some flew, some laid hands on their state maps and prayed.

Second, at the end of three days a team should visit each state capitol building, pray on the steps and "plant the Word" by literally burying somewhere on the capitol grounds a paper having this Scripture written on it: "Every place that the sole of your foot will tread upon, I have given you" (Josh. 1:3).

The initiative was launched by a 24-hour prayer watch on August 21, 1992. Special prayer meetings were to be held August 24 and 25, then August 26 was the day of the multi-faceted prayer expedition covering the entire nation. After it was done, the report said, "Every state in the United States has been 'claimed' for God's purposes and it was declared to the enemy that this land belongs to God—He is the ruler, yet!"

WHAT DO PRAYER EXPEDITIONS PRAY FOR?

The London to Berlin prayer expedition covered 28 segments in 31 days. The route was carefully laid out and an expedition manual listed key prayer points for every day. The manual was also distributed to intercessors and prayer teams that stayed home, but who agreed to pray daily for those on the expedition itself.

Each of the 28 segments of the manual included:

- A general prayer suggestion for the team appropriate to that specific day.
- Items for thanksgiving and praise including Scriptures to be prayed back to God.
- A specific prayer focus for the day.
- Several "key prayer points."

Expedition Mapping

The key prayer points of the expedition manual did not come easily. They emerged through careful spiritual mapping. Some elementary spiritual mapping is helpful, but not a prerequisite for praise marches and prayerwalks. However, the effectiveness of a prayer expedition will often be determined by the skill of the spiritual mappers who participate in giving direction to the participants.

Following the lead of today's ranking, spiritual-mapping expert, George Otis Jr., we describe spiritual mapping as an attempt to see our city (or whatever) as it *really is*, not as it *appears to be*. We attempt to get behind what is visible and discern the invisible, both good and evil, behind it. The concept is predicated on the biblical concept of a hierarchy of principalities and powers operating under the central command of Satan to prevent God from being glorified in the world. (See Dan. 10:13,20; Matt. 25:41; Eph. 3:10; 6:12; Col. 2:15; cf. Rev. 9:11.) To the degree that the powers, or territorial spirits, can be identified and unmasked, our prayers for a city or a neighborhood or a region presumably can be more accurately targeted. (Compare Eph. 6:12 and Rom. 15:30; Col. 4:12.)

Spiritual mapping first seeks to discover God's "redemptive gift" for the city. John Dawson says, "Determining your city's redemptive gift is even more important than discerning the nature of evil principalities. Principalities rule through perverting the gift of a city in the same way an individual's gift is turned to the enemy's use through sin."[7] When a prayer expedition approaches a given city, it is important to ask, "Why is this city here? If God's Kingdom were to come in full, what unique contribution would this city be asked to make?"

This is the positive starting point for spiritual mapping. But it is important also to discover Satan's strongholds in the city. Cindy Jacobs describes nine different kinds of strongholds: personal strongholds, strongholds of the mind, ideological strongholds, occultic strongholds, social strongholds, strongholds between city and church, seats of Satan, sectarian strongholds and strongholds of iniquities.[8] Satan's influence in a city can be weakened by tearing down the strongholds that give him a legal right to perpetuate evil in the city (cf. 2 Cor. 2:10,11; Eph. 4:26,27; Rev. 2:9,13), and the more we know about the strongholds the more precisely we can target our intercession against them.

Providing ongoing support for some of the strongholds of the enemy are corporate sins of the city, both past and present, which have not yet been remitted. I have written more extensively on this in another book in this series, *Warfare Prayer.*[9] In yet another book in this series, *Breaking Strongholds in Your City*, I have provided a list of 60 questions (see chapter 9) that can be helpful in getting to the root of things as they *really are* in a city. Three approaches need to be taken: historical research, physical research and spiritual research.

When put together with the help of seasoned intercessors and those who have spiritual gifts of discernment of spirits, the information gathered can be of immense usefulness to those

---

Spiritual mapping does for intercessors what X rays do for a physician.

---

who are moving along in a prayer expedition. Spiritual mapping does for intercessors what X rays do for a physician.

Key Prayer Points
The spiritual mapping done for the "key prayer points" in the 28 segments of the London to Berlin prayer expedition is most impressive. As I read them, however, I cannot help but think that perhaps in as little as a couple of years from now we will regard them as good, but quite elementary. At one time, typewriters were considered state of the art, but no longer with the advent of electronic word processors. I am confident that spir-

itual mapping in the future will be much more sophisticated
·than anything we know today.

What do I mean? Here are some of the concrete examples
from the London to Berlin *Prayer Diary.*

• On Sunday, April 26 the expedition moves from Dover,
England to Calais, France. Calais is the location of the famous
Notre Dame Cathedral where they will hold a concert of prayer
that night with Christians from both Britain and France. In
Calais they are to direct their prayers toward:

1. Humiliation: The symbol of the town is a statue with six
   burghers (local residents), ropes around their necks and
   heads bowed. On August 3, 1342, Edward III, King of
   England, ordered that six of the most prominent men of
   the town give themselves up and leave the town to
   offer him the town keys. They were forced to go bare-
   footed and with halters around their necks.
2. Strong powers: A winged dragon dominates the top of
   the town hall clock. In most French towns there is a
   rooster, not a dragon!

• On Friday, May 15 the group travels from Hanover to
Braunschweig, Germany. By way of background, Adolf Hitler
became a German citizen in the city of Braunschweig. Under
his direction, the main cathedral was taken over by the SS and
used for schooling SS officers. Hitler found tremendous support from the people of Braunschweig, without any significant
objection from the State Church. At present, Braunschweig has
the lowest church attendance of any Germany city. Pray:

1. Against the forces of Freemasonry.
2. Against the spirits of division that contest every step
   taken toward unity among believers and their respective fellowships.

3. Against spirits of distrust that Satan uses to extinguish the flow of God's love among His children.

• Morsleben, Germany: The only place in Germany where, until recently, nuclear waste could be taken. There is a stronghold of death. It is a meeting place for many neo-Nazis. The few Christians there are called a sect and seriously attacked by sicknesses.

• Erxleben, Germany: Pray against unemployment in the area. About 50 percent of the population are unemployed.

• Magdeburg, Germany: Pray against the spirit of death, which is very strong. Often children or young people die unnaturally. The Autobahn (superhighway) is the one with the most accidents in Germany and many people have died there.

WHO GOES ON PRAYER EXPEDITIONS?

It is obvious that not every Christian will feel called to invest the time, energy and money in participating in a prayer expedition. The need for maturity, commitment and specific divine calling is higher than in praise marches and prayerwalks. Each prayer expedition team should have a reasonable number of experienced, gifted intercessors and all need to be accustomed to participating in sustained prayer.

It would be foolish to launch out on a prayer expedition without sufficient accompanying intercession. Each member of the team should be required to recruit intercessors who stay home but who will promise to pray daily. The London to Berlin *Prayer Diary* is appropriately designed to help them do this intelligently.

The *Prayer Diary* lists the names of 54 people who committed to participate in all or part of the London to Berlin expedition along with 8 others as support personnel. To involve more believers, on 21 of the 30 nights of the expedition they scheduled beforehand a concert of prayer with the Christians of the town in which they arrived. In many of the towns, the local Christians became very enthusiastic and crowds of up to 400 would welcome them at their town lines as they walked in.

The Women's Aglow "Casting a Net of Prayer" expedition in the United States used mostly automobiles as transportation. The report says, "From Mount Denali in Alaska to New Jersey shores, yellow ribbons tied to cars or worn as arm bands were a symbol of Christ's love surrounding women as they covered their areas with 'prayer nets.'"

In both Louisiana and Florida, women drove the coastline all day and stopped every 7 miles to pray. In California, teams drove from east to west and from north to south, crossing the state with prayer. They said, "It was like tying a ribbon on a package." One lady in Virginia drove 20 hours in 3 days. Another group in Virginia chartered an airplane and covered the state from the border of North Carolina to the border of West Virginia with prayer.

In Japan, Paul K. Ariga, national coordinator of the Spiritual Warfare Network, organized a railroad prayer expedition. A Christian railroad executive assisted them in leasing a train that had 6 passenger cars, and 400 pray-ers volunteered to travel together to 6 cities in the Osaka area, praying and praising inside the train as they rode along, and outside the train as they stopped in the cities. Ariga later leased a ferryboat carrying 1,000 for a day's prayer expedition around the Osaka harbor.

In 1992, David Bryant and Jeff Marks of Concerts of Prayer organized 12 leaders of churches in New England for a prayer expedition covering 5 states. They traveled more than 800 miles in 2 RVs and a Toyota. In a period of 78 hours they participated in 4 concerts of prayer and 9 pastor/leader prayer meetings. New England may well lead the way toward revival for all of the United States.

THE REASON FOR PRAYER EXPEDITIONS

The reason for prayer expeditions can be stated quite simply: to open a given region spiritually for the Kingdom of God.

When we pray, "Thy kingdom come, thy will be done, on earth as it is in heaven" (Matt. 6:10, *NASB*), we can rightly expect God to move. In this case, He moves in the hearts of His people to use prayer as the principal weapon of spiritual warfare out there where obviously God's Kingdom is being resisted.

When we pray for God's Kingdom to come, what are we asking for? Specific answers to this are likely to vary from Christian group to Christian group. But where God's Kingdom is actually manifested and where His will is being done, we can agree across the board that there will be no war, murder and bloodshed; no poverty, starvation and misery; no unsaved souls; no greed, injustice and exploitation; no hate, prejudice and discrimination; no sickness, demonization and substance abuse; and there will be no sexual immorality, perversion and pornography.

KINGDOM MINISTRIES

Although I personally want *all* of God's Kingdom to come, my own calling is to give priority attention to evangelism. I have friends who also believe in evangelism, but they feel called to deal primarily with the murder of unborn babies. Others are wrapped up in feeding the hungry, delivering the demonized, reconciling the races or whatever else helps spread the will of God throughout society.

When I read Bill Wylie-Kellermann's *Seasons of Faith and Conscience*, I find that he is more concerned than some others in eliminating war as a means of settling human differences. I have never been inclined toward pacifism, but I am biblical enough to realize that a principal characteristic of God's Kingdom is peace and not violence.

I mention that because in his book Wylie-Kellermann sees prayer expeditions as a principal means of bringing peace and righteousness. For example, on Good Friday every year, 300 Christians do a prayer expedition through the streets of Detroit, Michigan, "pausing to pray at places where suffering is manifest (neighborhoods neglected and destroyed, the county jail, the site of a handgun shooting), where needs are ministered to (a soup kitchen, free health clinic, shelter for runaways) or decisions made (city-county building, the Federal building)."[10] I have no doubt that those on the London to Berlin prayer expedition or the Aglow women would have chosen similar targets for their prayers.

The real battle for both world evangelization and social justice is a spiritual battle and our principal weapon of spiritual warfare is prayer.

In March 1992, a prayer expedition was held in the Philippines called "March for Life 1992," tracing the 93-mile route of the infamous Bataan Death March forced upon American and Filipino prisoners by the Japanese during World War II. Of the 70,000 forced to march, 10,000 lost their lives. A Japanese pastor proposed the prayer expedition, and as a part of it Japanese leaders publicly repented of the cruel sins of the Japanese soldiers and asked forgiveness. Americans asked forgiveness for the atomic holocaust of Hiroshima. Special additional points of prayer included the terrible debt forced upon the Philippines by the Bataan Nuclear Power Plant built by Westinghouse under the corrupt Marcos government, for the destruction caused by the Mount Pinatubo eruption, and for the economic devastation in the areas being vacated by United States military bases.[11]

As I have said earlier, it is fascinating to see how the Spirit of God is speaking to the wider Body of Christ these days when we mutually begin to realize that the real battle for both world evangelization and social justice is a spiritual battle and that our principal weapon of spiritual warfare is prayer. We begin to recognize that the real enemy is the devil and not each other. I was intrigued to see that in his excellent book, *Engaging the Powers*, Walter Wink discusses both Peter Wagner and Bill Wylie-Kellermann in the same paragraph and says, "I sense here a convergence of aims that may have the disconcerting result of linking charismatics, conservative evangelicals, and social-action liberals in a united front of enormous power."[12]

HOW DO WE PRAY?

Four major kinds of prayer characterize prayer expeditions:

1. Prayers of repentance. Gwen Shaw repented of the sins of her ancestors in persecuting fellow believers. Japanese Christians repented of the sins of their military forces in the Bataan Death March. The Scripture says, "If My people who are called by My name will humble themselves" (2 Chron. 7:14). Humility and repentance are among God's requirements for His response in "healing their land."

2. Prayers of intercession. The Lord said, "I sought for a man among them who would make a wall, and stand in the gap before Me on behalf of the land" (Ezek. 22:30). Participants in prayer expeditions feel a responsibility to stand in the gap for the land through which they are traveling. Through intercession, they beseech God to reveal to them the strongholds of the enemy in each place they visit and to show them His strategy for pulling down the strongholds as they are commanded to do in 2 Corinthians 10:4,5.

3. Prayers of proclamation. Announcing out loud the glory and majesty of God is both a privilege and responsibility of the pray-ers. "Among the gods there is none like You, O Lord; nor are there any works like Your works. All nations whom You have made shall come and worship before You, O Lord" (Ps. 86:8,9). This is often done through singing and at times shouting.

4. Prayers of blessing. Individuals need healing. Families need healing. Towns and cities need healing. Centers of political, economic, military and religious power need healing. Lost souls need to be saved. A large part of prayer-expedition praying pleads with God for blessing on the land and the people.

WHERE DO WE GO FROM HERE?

If prayer expeditions can truly help to open regions for the coming of the Kingdom of God, the possibilities for developing them are enormous.

I was deeply moved when I recently talked to Lynn Green of YWAM, one of the London group giving much support to prayer expeditions. He has an unusual burden, as do many today, for seeing Muslims come under God's blessing through Jesus Christ. I also believe we are on the verge of seeing an enormous spiritual harvest among Muslims. But if a massive turning point is to come, I believe it will only happen with some cataclysmic spiritual victory in the invisible world.

Lynn Green said, "I wonder what it would look like if we were able some day to mobilize thousands of Christians who would commit themselves to do prayer expeditions simultaneously along every route of the crusades. We would have them start in every city and town where crusades originated, follow the routes, converge in Istanbul and walk to Jerusalem. There would be only one agenda item: sincere, public repentance for the sins committed by Christians against Muslims and Jews." In fact, a beginning event was held in Jerusalem in 1993.

There would be no lack of sins and iniquities for which to repent if adequate spiritual mapping were done. I heard of one city in Germany, for example, in which the Christian leaders financed their crusade by confiscating the material goods of 500 Jewish families. It is said that Bernard of Clairvaux preached: "To arms then! Let a holy indignation animate you to combat, and let the cry of Jeremiah reverberate through Christendom: Cursed be he that withholds his sword from blood!"[13] When we read such things we no longer wonder why Muslim leaders call American presidents "The Great Satan." And why Muslim rulers declare that Christianity is out of bounds for their citizens.

International politics, economic summits and Desert Storms cannot do any more than make cosmetic adjustments in the status quo because the real battle for the Muslim world is in the invisible arena, which the United Nations knows nothing about. But Lynn Green and prayer leaders like him know much about it, and know that without repentance and the shedding of blood there is no remittance of sin. The blood of Jesus Christ has been shed, and only Spirit-led repentance in God's time and on a God-size scale will begin to open the way for it to be applied as God desires.

I personally believe that by having the kind of a prayer expedition Lynn Green envisions, the Muslim world could be permanently broken open for the blessing of God to pour upon them.

■ REFLECTION QUESTIONS ■

1. Think of walking and praying for 30 days from London to

Berlin. What sort of people would undertake such a thing? Would you be excited to take part in something like that?

2. Why do you think members of Women's Aglow Fellowship would actually bury Bible verses in the grounds of state capitols? Is there any biblical precedence for such prophetic prayer actions?

3. "Spiritual mapping" may be a new term for you. If so, list some of the benefits it could have for targeting prayer more precisely. For more information on spiritual mapping, be sure to get the previous book in this *Prayer Warrior* series, *Breaking Strongholds in Your City*.

4. In most prayer expeditions, prayers of repentance are featured. Review the chapter and see if you can name four or five specific examples. Why is this so important?

5. Consider Lynn Green's proposal for prayer expeditions dealing with the crusades. What is your opinion? Could other prominent iniquities be dealt with in a similar way? How about slavery and racism?

Notes

1. Prayerwalking formerly was a generic term covering what we now distinguish more accurately as prayerwalks, prayer expeditions and prayer journeys.

2. Graham Kendrick and John Houghton, *Prayerwalking* (Eastbourne, England: Kingsway Publications, 1990), p. 37.

3. Graham Kendrick, Gerald Coates, Roger Forster and Lynn Green with Catherine Butcher, *March for Jesus* (Eastbourne, England: Kingsway Publications, 1992), pp. 56-59.

4. Gwen Shaw, *End-Time Handmaidens Newsletter* (P.O. Box 447, Jasper, AR 72641), October 1992, p. 1.

5. Ibid., p. 4.

6. Kendrick, et. al., *March for Jesus*, pp. 113,114.

7. John Dawson, *Taking Our Cities for God* (Lake Mary, FL: Creation House, 1989), p. 41.

8. Cindy Jacobs, "Dealing with Strongholds," *Breaking Strongholds in Your City*, C. Peter Wagner, ed. (Ventura, CA: Regal Books, 1993), pp. 71-95.

9. C. Peter Wagner, *Warfare Prayer* (Ventura, CA: Regal Books, 1992), chapter 7 "Remitting the Sins of Nations."

10. Bill Wylie-Kellermann, *Seasons of Faith and Conscience* (Maryknoll, NY: Orbis Books, 1991), p. xxv.

11. Kathryn J. Johnson, "Marching for Life in the Philippines," *The Christian Century,* June 3-10, 1992, pp. 573,574.
12. Walter Wink, *Engaging the Powers* (Minneapolis, MN: Fortress Press, 1992), p. 314.
13. Quoted in Marvin E. Tate's, "War and Peacemaking in the Old Testament," *Review and Expositor,* Fall 1982, p. 589.

Prayer Journeys

H AROLD CABALLEROS IS PASTOR OF THE 4,000-MEMBER EL
Shaddai Church in Guatemala City and also one of
the top-ranking leaders of the Spiritual Warfare Network. For some time he has known what it means to
pray outside the church and in the community.

GUATEMALA AT A CROSSROADS

In 1990 Guatemala was at a political crossroads. The
evangelical church had grown rapidly in that nation
until about 30 percent of the population were evangelical Christians, the highest percentage in Latin America.
Christians all over the nation were praying for righteousness and justice in their nation, and the national
elections were coming up in 1991.

It happened that one of the presidential candidates,
Jorge Serrano Elías, was an active member of El Shaddai

Church. Naturally, his brothers and sisters in Christ prayed with him as he entered the political race. He had previously run in 1986, while part of a different church, and had lost. El Shaddai is a church that has been trained in two-way prayer, and through prayer God gave them a prophetic message that Serrano Elías was going to be president of Guatemala. Taking the word from the Lord seriously, they prayed that God's will would be done and that Serrano Elías would win the election.

God had been leading Harold Caballeros in high-level spiritual warfare. A year or two previously they had purchased land for their church bordered at the back by a 20-foot mound of dirt. They later discovered that this was a section of a 14-mile-long image of a Mayan spirit, Quetzacoatl, the feathered serpent. It had been built in pre-Colombian days and its Mayan origin had not been recognized by archaeologists until the 1960s. Harold began to lead the El Shaddai congregation in serious spiritual warfare against the spirits behind the serpent.

Nationwide Spiritual Warfare
In 1990, Caballeros began to sense that God was calling his church to enter into nationwide spiritual warfare to clear the way spiritually as much as possible before the elections. He decided to organize prayer journeys as the vehicle for this.

The church recruited 66 of the their most gifted and seasoned intercessors for the journey. They needed 3 intercessors for each of the 22 departments (states) of Guatemala. After the intercessors met with each other to receive training and pray together, each team went to the capital city of the department, put up in a hotel, and was to stay there and pray as long as necessary until they sensed a spiritual breakthrough.

Many positive results came out of these simultaneous prayer journeys. The governor of one of the departments said, "The prayers of these three ladies have literally changed the history of my department. God's blessing is now with us." The governor as well recognized that history belongs to the intercessors, as Walter Wink would say.

As the intercessors returned to the church, some of them brought fascinating reports. Among other things, they had identified three powerful human beings who were being used by the spiritual forces of darkness as strongmen. Two of them were presidential candidates, and both had higher ratings in the polls than Jorge Serrano Elías. In fact, Serrano Elías was so low in the polls at that time that few were taking his candidacy seriously. Many times the media would not include him in the list of potential candidates.

The Three Strongmen
The first candidate was a drug king who had powerful vested interests supporting his candidacy. The intercessors prayed that his campaign would not prosper. Soon after the prayer journey he held a meeting of his closest supporters, most of whom carried guns. As a precaution, all were required to leave their guns on a table in the room while the meeting was in session. But a woman who was arranging the guns on the table accidentally dropped one that fired, and the bullet seriously wounded the presidential candidate. His family had to fly him to Houston, Texas, where he underwent surgery and later regained full health. But meanwhile he had to drop out of the electoral race!

The second candidate was the mayor of the capital city of the department in which the intercessors were praying. Within a week of the church's prayer journey, the mayor was taken into custody by the police as a drug dealer. They uncovered large amounts of drugs, huge quantities of cash in United States dollars and a warehouse full of stolen cars. When this became known, the members of his party were so incensed that they voted for Serrano Elías, not so much because they favored him, but because they wanted to defeat their former candidate.

The third strongman identified by the prayer journeys was not a drug dealer, but was a leader who promoted violence. The El Shaddai church also prayed against the spirits of violence that controlled him.

The result was that Jorge Serrano Elías was elected president by a record-breaking 67 percent of the votes on the first ballot, one of the rare times that a runoff election was not needed in a multiparty campaign.

Prayer journeys primarily focus on strongholds. A stronghold is a set of circumstances in the context of human life that furnish demonic principalities and powers a legal base on which to establish a center of operations.

At this writing the president, along with the vice president who is also a believer, has been meeting twice a year for a 9:00 A.M. to 2:00 P.M. prayer meeting with 1,800 to 2,000 of Guatemala's pastors. He says there is a long way to go before the justice and righteousness they are praying for fully characterize the nation, but they all feel that important steps are being taken in that direction.

PRAYER JOURNEYS FOCUS ON STRONGHOLDS

Praise marches focus on cities, prayerwalks focus on neighborhoods and prayer expeditions focus on regions, but prayer journeys primarily focus on strongholds.

A stronghold is a set of circumstances in the context of human life that furnish demonic principalities and powers a legal base on which to establish a center of operations. Cindy Jacobs defines a stronghold as "a fortified place which Satan builds to exalt himself against the knowledge and plans of God."[1]

The apostle Paul says, "The weapons of our warfare are not carnal but mighty in God for pulling down strongholds, casting down arguments and every high thing that exalts itself against the knowledge of God, bringing every thought into captivity to the obedience of Christ" (2 Cor. 10:4,5). This passage hints of four kinds of strongholds:

1. Sectarian strongholds. "Casting down arguments" (v. 5). A fairly large number of Christians like to argue. The nature of arguments is to prove your position is right, and of course one tried-and-true way of attempting that is to prove the person who disagrees with you is wrong. I am rather amazed at the considerable number of articles as well as books that are being written, arguing that some of the things I am saying about prayer in this *Prayer Warrior* series are wrong. A friend of mine who does much of this writing told me, "I believe my calling is that of a polemicist." He cannot understand how I can quote with approval some of the things a person such as, for example, Walter Wink might say while not also raising other issues on which we disagree and refuting his position. He wants me to make myself look good by making others look bad.

Polemics rarely persuade others that they should change their minds and become more like you. More frequently they cause the others to harden their opinion and widen the gap. This is precisely the cause of much of the division in the Body of Christ today. We must never compromise on the essential biblical principles concerning the person and work of Jesus Christ ("one Lord, one faith" [Eph. 4:2-5]). But there is lots of room for both disagreement and mutual respect on secondary doctrines Much of our Christian polemics, I am afraid, constitute strongholds for the enemy.

2. Occultic strongholds. "Every high thing that exalts itself against the knowledge of God" (v. 5). The Greek for "high thing" is *hypsoma*, which *The New International Dictionary of New Testament Theology* says, "probably reflects astrological ideas, and hence denotes cosmic powers...powers directed against God, seeking to intervene between God and man."[2] Cindy Jacobs says, "The territorial spirits over a city or region are greatly empowered by the occult spells, curses, rituals and fetishes used by witches, warlocks, and satanists."[3] When Harold Caballeros discovered the Mayan feathered serpent in the backyard of his church, he began to uncover some occultic strongholds, which were subsequently weakened.

3. Strongholds of the mind. "Bringing every thought into captivity" (v. 5). Many have criticized Robert Schuller for teaching "possibility thinking," but I have personally found that attempting to cast my thoughts and plans in a positive light has helped my ministry and my own personal well-being greatly. My friend Edgardo Silvoso has said on many an occasion, "A stronghold is a mind-set impregnated with hopelessness that causes the believer to accept as unchangeable something he or she knows is contrary to the will of God." Both Schuller and Silvoso are describing biblical faith, without which it is impossible to please God (see Heb. 11:6).

Lack of faith is a stronghold of the mind that Satan uses. Jesus was exasperated with it enough to exclaim to His disciples more than once, "O you of little faith!"

4. Personal strongholds. "The obedience of Christ,...being ready to punish all disobedience" (2 Cor. 10:5,6). Any lowering of standards of obedience or holiness in the lives of believers furnishes a springboard for Satan. If we are going to "resist the devil" as James says, we must also "draw near to God" (Jas. 4:7,8). Among other things, this means that we must "cleanse our hands" and "purify our hearts." Either wrong actions or wrong motives or a combination of the two can give Satan personal strongholds and a legal right to do his evil work.

These four do not exhaust the list of possible strongholds, but they do give concrete examples of some of the things God desires us to "pull down." An important part of prayer journeys is to do that very thing, thereby setting free the ministries of evangelism and social action that follow.

TWO KINDS OF PRAYER JOURNEYS

Experience to date has indicated that it is helpful to distinguish between two kinds of prayer journeys. One is called "intercessory prayer journeys" and the other "prophetic prayer journeys." Both are rather advanced forms of praying in the community, but prophetic prayer journeys are the most advanced. Compared to other kinds of praying outside the church, which may be seen as primary and secondary school, intercessory prayer journeys are like college and prophetic prayer journeys like graduate school.

The devil is very jealous of making sure that the strongholds he is currently using are securely maintained. Prayer journeys are a direct, overt threat to the enemy's well-being, and he will do everything possible to oppose them. I say this not to instill fear because "greater is he that is within you, than he that is in the world" (1 John 4:4, *KJV*), but I say it to encourage an appropriate degree of caution. Joining Marches for Jesus and most prayerwalks is one thing, but engaging the enemy in prayer journeys is quite something else. Planning a prayer journey is a declaration of war against Satan.

INTERCESSORY PRAYER JOURNEYS

To conduct an intercessory prayer journey, a given church or ministry recruits a prayer team of, say, 5 to 10 members, and sends them to another city or other strategic point for the purpose of on-site prayer.

The Asian Outreach ministry in Hong Kong recently sent a team of 4 intercessors to Da Nang, Vietnam, for a prayer journey. When they disembarked from their 30-hour train ride, they had no specific plans. But they did have a purpose. "We had come to Danang with one specific goal in mind," says Cao An Dien, one of the intercessors. "We had come here to pray."[4] She says they did not know where in Vietnam the Lord would lead them when they left Hong Kong, but "as we prayed for the cities of Vietnam, we sensed a darkness about Danang, as if there was something significant to pray about."[5]

As they began exploring and looking for prayer targets the first day, they stopped for breakfast in a small restaurant. The restaurant's chef, a Chinese Vietnamese named Trung, told them he was holding down 3 jobs so he could save enough money to escape Vietnam. They did not have a chance to present the gospel to him, but they did pray for him often while they were in Danang. They prayed for the city, they prayed against the strongholds they could discern, they prayed for the 67 unreached people groups in Vietnam, they prayed for the persecuted Christians there and they prayed for the individual people they encountered day by day.

Eight months later they were thrilled when one of their team who was ministering in a Vietnamese camp back in Hong Kong ran into Trung! She then shared the gospel with him and left a devotional book for him, written in English and Chinese. Six months later they found him again. This time he was radiant. "I have become a Christian," he beamed. "Through reading this devotional book I have come to know Jesus as my Lord and Savior."[6]

And Danang? Did the prayer journey have an effect? Cao An Dien says, "In the months following our visit there, it was reported that the church in Danang was discovering greater freedom since the government was no longer clamping down as they had before. Many were being saved in this city." Then she adds something very important for prayer warriors to keep in mind: "The Lord was answering not only our prayers but also those of many others who were upholding this city in prayer."[7]

Praying Through the Window

During the month of October 1993, the same month this book is due to be released, the most massive international prayer event in memory will be under way. Called "Praying Through the Window," it is sponsored by the A.D. 2000 Movement United Prayer Track and coordinated by Dick Eastman of Every Home for Christ and Jane Hansen of Women's Aglow. Christians all over the world will be challenged to make a special effort to pray for the unreached peoples and the unevangelized cities of the 10/40 Window.

"10/40 WINDOW"

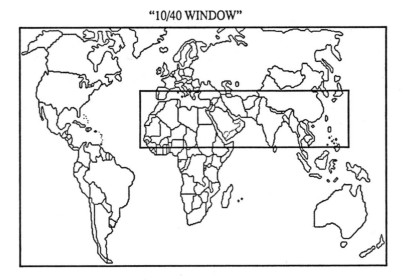

Millions of intercessors are being lined up to pray through the month of October. At this writing some bold goals have been set:

- Women's Aglow International hopes to mobilize 500,000 women to pray through the month.
- William Kumuyi hopes to enlist up to 2 million Africans from more than 40 nations.
- The Korean A.D. 2000 committee is fairly sure they will have 1 million Koreans praying specifically for the 10/40 Window.

The idea of filling public stadiums has been suggested by the Japanese. The United Prayer Track representative, Paul K. Ariga, is working with the organizing committee of the All-Japan Revival Koshien Mission, which has leased the famous Koshien baseball stadium for 3 nights. Leading up to this, Ariga is also promoting 180,000 hours of intercessory prayer. Because they hope to fill the 60,000-seat stadium all 3 nights, a total of 180,000 seats will be occupied. To provide 1 hour of prayer for each seat, Ariga has more than 7,000 Japanese believers committed to pray and fast and send in a postcard whenever they have completed 10 hours of prayer. The numbers are all computerized and monitored.

Many Christian leaders in other countries are planning to follow the lead of the Japanese, at least for one night, in some cases Halloween night, October 31, 1993.

Two Hundred Forty-eight Prayer Journeys

Not only does this initiative desire to pray *for* the 10/40 Window, but it is also planning prayer *in* the 10/40 Window through at least 248 intercessory prayer journeys. The number 248 is derived from multiplying the 62 nations of the greater 10/40 Window targeted for prayer by the 4 weeks in October.

Plans are to have a prayer team in each of the 62 nations (or in some cases it may have to be at the border) each of the 4 weeks in the month. Several will meet with on-site partisan prayer teams.

Only the Lord knows if any or all of these goals and other goals that may subsequently emerge will be fully or partially met. In any case, the vision for synchronizing prayer journeys is a cutting-edge concept worthy of experimentation.

The prayer journeys are being coordinated by Ted Haggard, pastor of the New Life Church of Colorado Springs, Colorado, who has organized a new ministry for this enterprise called Christian Information Network. Haggard's assignment is to see that four teams are assigned to each country, one week each. It is hoped that the prayer teams will come from many nations of the world, and given the visa restrictions on many of the 10/40 Window nations, Ted will make sure that teams from appropriate nations will be assigned to limited-access countries.

The spiritual mapping will be provided by the Spiritual Mapping Division of the United Prayer Track under George Otis Jr. Otis says, "We must find a way to lift the enchantment of the enemy over the hearts and minds of resident people groups. Accomplishing this task—which the Bible defines as binding the strongman (Matt. 12:29)—requires both an accurate identification of our spiritual competition, and the faith and commitment to persevere in prayer."[8]

Otis's team is committed to researching and distributing what they call "targeting coordinates," dealing with specific spiritual strongholds of every kind for each of the 62 nations that will receive intercessors. Furthermore, he has worked with Dick Eastman to produce a generic prayer guide for the month, which outlines general ways of day-by-day praying for the 62 nations.

Training for Prayer Journeys
Training for intelligent, strategic-warfare prayer will be provid-

ed to those who volunteer for the intercessory prayer journeys. A video conference featuring Luis Bush, Peter Wagner, Dick Eastman, David Bryant, Cindy Jacobs, George Otis Jr. and Ted Haggard is available from the Christian Information Network. Otis is producing a training manual called *Strongholds of the 10/40 Window* (The Sentinel Group), which will include instructions on understanding strongholds, identifying strongholds and responding to strongholds. Many are also using my books *Warfare Prayer* and *Breaking Strongholds in Your City* and Cindy Jacobs' *Possessing the Gates of the Enemy* (Chosen Books).

The cost of sending 248 teams of 5 to 10 each to Southeast Asia, North Africa, India, the Himalayas, Japan or other 10/40 Window destinations is considerable. And this raises an interesting question for church and ministry leaders: How important is prayer for effective evangelism? Most Christian leaders will say, "Prayer is number one," but as I remarked in chapter 2, much of this turns out to be mere rhetoric. Nothing demonstrates people's real level of commitment more than their willingness to commit money.

Depending on many factors, it could cost a church between $10,000 and $25,000 to send an intercessory prayer team to the 10/40 Window. This, I realize, is enough to give many pastors sticker shock. However, I also believe that 248 churches or ministries from many nations regard warfare prayer strongly enough to commit the funds. One church in Guatemala has already signed up and is believing God that the funds will be there when the time comes and that their team will go. Another team from American Navajo Indians has committed themselves to the prayer journey.

Those who volunteer for an intercessory prayer journey must realize that they are not going on a vacation. It will not be a week or 10 days of fun and games. It will be an authentic venture in short-term, cross-cultural missions. An advantage they have is that they will not have to learn a language because they can pray in their native tongue. But in many cases the food will be substandard; they will be plagued by nuisance illnesses such as diarrhea and colds; jet lag will throw their systems out of kilter; accommodations in some cases will be Spartan, having few comforts of home. And as this is overt spiritual warfare, challenging areas of deep and long-standing demonic entrenchment, there will inevitably be casualties. It is not a job for the fainthearted, but for those few who are called, strengthened and empowered by the almighty God.

The results can be radical changes in the balance of power in the heavenlies and an outpouring of the Kingdom of God in lands previously enslaved to darkness.

PROPHETIC PRAYER JOURNEYS

I imagine that the percentage of Christians who engage in prophetic prayer journeys, compared to intercessory prayer journeys, would be about that of high-school athletes who eventually compete in the Olympic Games.

Although the concept of prophetic prayer journeys is new to many of us, it is not new to Swedish intercessor Kjell Sjöberg. Kjell (pronounced "Shell") is one of those spiritual Olympic athletes, so to speak, who has garnered as much experience as anyone in this exacting ministry. In his book, *Winning the Prayer War*, he says that they have "confirmed that individuals exist today with a gift for prophetic espionage. Certain people who have experienced God's holiness and His steadfast love, while in worship before Him, have been given a hunting instinct to track down the enemy's manipulations. Evil is something that we can localize and give a name to."[9]

Sjöberg believes that prayer journeys should be used much more than they have been in preparing the way for evangelism. He says, "A hundred years ago, when missionaries were being mobilized to go to China and other lands with the Gospel, the prayer supporters were told to stay at home and support those who went to fight in the front line. I believe we can do better than this today, and I say to the intercessors, 'You go in first, and clear the way for the evangelists and those who plant new churches!'"[10]

In his book, Sjöberg, who says he has been called to "take prayer teams to hard, difficult places, closed lands, and unreached peoples,"[11] tells of prophetic prayer journeys to cities such as Paris, Brussels, Bonn, Warsaw and Athens. He speaks of strongholds he has encountered such as Mammon, the Harlot, Materialism, Fatherlessness, Death, Conspiracy and many others. And then he speaks of spiritual victories.

For example, he tells of a prayer journey to Budapest where they identified the strongman over Hungary as a spirit of slavery. They prayed very specifically to cast out that territorial spirit of slavery. "The answer to our prayer came," he says, "when, two years later, the barbed wire around the borders was cut down and sold as souvenirs, and Hungarians could travel freely to other countries once more."[12]

In Paris they sensed they needed to combat the spirit of revolution, and particularly came against the May Day demonstrations. "Since we prayed there," Sjöberg says, "the May Day celebrations in the former communist and socialist countries have lost their power to attract the crowds."[13]

Prophetic Prayer Acts

Those who follow the activities of prophetic intercessors are at times puzzled by some of their behavior. Some of the things they do appear to be irrational, or even bizarre. Sadly, some immature and unwise enthusiasts do commit stupid acts that are not of the Holy Spirit. But those intercessors who are truly in touch with God are, at times, asked to do strange things. Kjell Sjöberg says, "Prophetic prayer actions are done only at the Lord's command in God's perfect timing according to a strategy that the Lord has revealed for the team."[14]

For example, my friend Filiberto Lemus, who pastors a rural church in western Guatemala, is also a recognized intercessor. At a recent Spiritual Warfare Network meeting he told of how things had not been going well at his church because of severe opposition to the gospel from the townspeople. As he was praying over this, God gave him some rather strange instructions. At 4:00 o'clock one morning, when the town was still asleep, his church members were to gather in three groups around the town, and conduct simultaneous torch marches through the streets of the town, ending at the church for prayer. From the date of that prophetic prayer act, attendance in his church has increased dramatically.

Kjell Sjöberg tells of a group of intercessors led to do a prophetic prayer act in the desert near Bersheva (Beersheba), Israel. They took along two sticks. On one stick they wrote, "For Judah and the children of Israel," and on the other, "For Joseph, the stick of Ephraim." They bound the sticks together with a silver thread and joined them with a wedding ring. This was not their own idea. God had led them to reenact Ezekiel 37:16-22, praying fervently for unity between the radical Orthodox Jews and the secular Jews, and for harmony between Messianic Jews and other Jews.[15]

When we recall some of the God-directed behavior of Old Testament prophets, things come into perspective. Ezekiel had to lie on his left side for 390 days, then on his right side for 40 days (see Ezek. 4:4-6). He had to bake barley cakes using human dung as his fuel (see Ezek. 4:12,13). Jeremiah had to bury his underwear and later dig it up (see Jer. 13:1-7). Hosea had to marry a prostitute (see Hos. 1:2). And on and on. Their prophetic prayer acts must have seemed irrational and bizarre at the time, but we know from Scripture that they were in fact directions from the Lord.

Journeys to the Cardinal Points

Loren Cunningham, a leader for Youth With a Mission (YWAM), recently sensed that God was directing YWAM into a prophetic prayer strategy, which involved journeys to the world's cardinal points. They were impressed to do this after studying the significance of the "ends of the earth" in God's Word and particularly the invitation in Psalm 2:8: "Ask of me, and I will make the nations your inheritance, the ends of the earth your possession" *(NIV)*.

Roger McKnight, who now heads up YWAM International Prayer Events Coordination, was appointed to organize prayer teams to do on-site praying at the extreme north, south, east and west points of six continents. Choosing the technical geographic and cartographic term "cardinal points," the prayer initiative was called "Cardinal Points Prayer Strategy." Despite predictable logistical challenges and reports such as, "We felt that the enemy was contesting every mile we covered. It was a fight," 24 prayer teams were in place and in prayer on September 21, 1991.

Now having joined the A.D. 2000 United Prayer Track, and having more support from the worldwide Body of Christ, Roger McKnight's vision has expanded. As a part of the Day to Change the World on June 25, 1994, he hopes to not only organize prophetic prayer journeys in a "second wave" to the same 24 continental cardinal points, but also to add the 4 cardinal points of as many individual nations of the world as he can on the same day.

This kind of prayer action sounds so unconventional some will be asking, "What good could something like this possibly do?" The same question was probably being asked by those observing Jesus mix up spit and dirt before anointing a blind man's eyes. It is the logic of the Kingdom of God.

Furthermore, most property owners inspect the boundaries

of their land or at least have their agents do it, or its inheritors. Inspections usually come when something significant is about

---

If God's salvation is to reach the "ends of the earth," then a prophetic prayer journey affirming God's dominion over "the world and those who dwell therein" may be unorthodox but certainly not invalid. It may be part of a plan orchestrated by God Himself, heralding a day of change for the world!

---

to happen to the property. In this light, if God's salvation is to reach the "ends of the earth" (Isa. 52:10), then a prophetic prayer journey affirming God's dominion over "the world and those who dwell therein" (Ps. 24:1) may be unorthodox but certainly not invalid. It may be part of a plan orchestrated by God Himself, heralding a day of change for the world! If God would have Jeremiah bury his underwear, He might also have prayer teams in Cabo Blanco, Brazil and Xaafun, Somalia and Cape Prince of Wales, Alaska, on June 25, 1994.

Praying Against War
Bill Wylie-Kellermann and a group of friends sensed the leading of the Lord for a prophetic prayer journey in 1983. This time they felt that God was leading them to pray against nuclear war and that their prophetic prayer act should take them to none other than Wurtsmith Air Force Base in northern Michigan, where 16 B-52s loaded with nuclear bombs were poised to take off on a moment's notice. They prayed for months previously to

seek the direction of God, then made their journey on Holy Saturday in 1983 to be on the base on Easter Sunday morning.

They prayed at 2:00 A.M. Easter Sunday, then began walking through the darkness toward the air force base in a wet snowstorm. When they reached the fence, they sensed they should do two prophetic acts: light the Paschal candle and cut the fence, and peacefully enter the air force base.

They reached the runway, prayed aloud to "renounce Satan and all his works," (see Rom. 13:12) and headed toward the brightly lighted area where the bombers were on alert. They arrived just as the sun was coming up and they expected to be apprehended. Vehicles were constantly patrolling, but Wylie-Kellermann reports, "Here an astonishing phenomenon occurred, one reportedly not uncommon in such undertakings. We passed unseen!"[16]

When they reached the high-security area, they knelt and took Holy Communion, asking God to prevent nuclear bombs from ever wiping out innocent human beings. They were surrounded by astounded and embarrassed armed guards before they finished, and allowed to finish their service with gospel songs of Resurrection. They expected to be arrested, but were only searched and dumped unceremoniously at the front gate without charges.

Who knows what the future holds? But we do know that since that prophetic prayer journey the danger of worldwide nuclear holocaust has measurably been less and less. So far the nuclear weapons have gone unused.

Code Words in Iraq

A fascinating prophetic prayer journey was led into Iraq by Kjell Sjöberg in 1990. My daughter Becky wrote it up for the *G.I. News*, newsletter of Generals of Intercession, and I will let her tell the story:

"In the summer of 1990, Kjell Sjöberg led fifteen men on a

ten-day prayer journey to Iraq. It was during the week they arrived that President Saddam Hussein had called an Arab summit meeting just prior to his invasion of Kuwait. As a result, the borders were closed to all tourist groups. Miraculously, Kjell's group was the only one allowed into the country.

"Because they arranged to visit a number of archaeological sites, their Iraqui tour guide mistook them for archaeologists and escorted them to every site they had targeted for prayer. Feeling as though they were being watched by secret police, the group arranged code words to use during their prayers. Israel was called "Michael's Land"; Saddam Hussein was "Hey man"; they called Muslims "musicians"; mission organizations were "companies"; and shouts of hallelujah to God were "Honolulu!"

"Kjell reported that their guide, named Mohammed Ali, shouted 'Honolulu!' just as much as the group of intercessors!

"History now reflects that the Arab summit coalition fell apart during the time that Kjell and his prayer group were in Iraq. Saddam Hussein was left by himself to invade Kuwait which eventually led to his defeat in war. The Lord already had His warriors behind enemy lines doing warfare in the heavenlies at what has proven to be a strategic time in history.

"Kjell Sjöberg and his men were surely not the only ones the Lord impressed to intercede that week over events in the Middle East, but we believe that their faithfulness to God's mandate did have some historical impact."[17]

So do I. I join Walter Wink and many others in declaring: *History belongs to the intercessors!*

▬ REFLECTION QUESTIONS ▬

1. Discuss the meaning of "stronghold" and give examples of the different kinds of strongholds that you yourself are aware of in your own church or community.

2. Sending 248 teams to pray in the "10/40 Window" for one week each will be very expensive. Is this a good cause of Christians' money or should it be spent on other things?
3. Do you feel that the concept of "prophetic espionage" is a valid one? What kind of a person do you think would be called to such a task? Are you acquainted with anyone who might fit the profile?
4. What are your feelings about the team that prayed inside Wurtsmith Air Force Base? How about those who prayed at the cardinal points of the earth in 1991? Are these actions too radical for most Christians to approve?
5. Can you arrive at any conclusions about what you, your friends and your church can do to implement praying *in* your community as well as praying *for* your community?

Notes
1. Cindy Jacobs, "Dealing with Strongholds," *Breaking Strongholds in Your City*, C. Peter Wagner, ed. (Ventura, CA: Regal Books, 1993), p. 80.
2. J. Blunck, "Height, Depth, Exalt," *The New International Dictionary of New Testament Theology*, Vol. 2, Colin Brown, ed. (Grand Rapids, MI: Zondervan Publishing House, 1976), p. 200.
3. Jacobs, "Dealing with Strongholds," p. 86.
4. Cao An Dien, "That God May Open a Door," *Asian Report*, May-June, 1992, p. 17.
5. Ibid.
6. Ibid., p. 20.
7. Ibid.
8. George Otis Jr., "Operation Second Chance" a privately circulated document by the Sentinel Group, 1992, p. 2.
9. Kjell Sjöberg, *Winning the Prayer War* (Chichester, England: New Wine Press, 1991), p. 60.
10. Ibid., p. 94.
11. Ibid.
12. Ibid., p. 76.
13. Ibid.
14. Kjell Sjöberg, "Spiritual Mapping for Prophetic Prayer Actions," *Breaking Strongholds in Your City*, C. Peter Wagner, ed. (Ventura, CA: Regal Books, 1993), p. 105.
15. Taken from the newsletter of Kjell and Lena Sjöberg, April 21, 1992.
16. Bill Wylie-Kellermann, *Seasons of Faith and Conscience* (Maryknoll, NY: Orbis Books, 1991), p. xxii.
17. Becky Wagner, "Profile of a General: Kjell Sjöberg," *G.I. News*, May-June 1992, p. 4.

CHURCHES INDEX THAT PRAY

   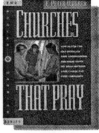